A CULINARY JOURNEY THROUGH

EAST

MALTA, LEBANON, IRAN, TURKEY,

WEST

MOROCCO, AND ANDALUSIA

Shane Delia

Interlink Books

An imprint of Interlink Publishing Group, Inc.
Northampton, Massachusetts

Introduction 8

Malta 10

Lebanon 24

Iran 68

Turkey 94

MOROCCO 162

ANDALUSIA 214
SPAIN

PANTRY 266
* pantry items are indicated
by an asterisk within recipes

INDEX 268

ABOUT THE AUTHOR

Shane Delia is the star of the television show *Shane Delia's Spice Journey*, and the chef and owner of Maha restaurant and Biggie Smalls Kebab Shop, both in Melbourne, Australia. He is a Western Bulldog Football Club, Melbourne City Football Club, Mercedes Benz Australia, and charity ambassador.

Shane's fun personality and enthusiasm for food and culture is captured in his acclaimed television show, which has aired in 135 countries across five continents and continues to be an international success.

Shane's flagship restaurant Maha has gone from strength to strength since its inception in 2008. Renowned for its fresh, unrestricted Middle Eastern menu, Maha has a style that is truly cutting edge. *The Age Good Food Guide* has continually recognized Maha as a leader in its field, awarding the restaurant One Chef Hat annually since 2009.

Shane is based in Melbourne. His wife Maha is the inspiration and namesake of his restaurant. Together they have two children, daughter Jayda and son Jude.

This is his second book.

INTRODUCTION

I'm sure you have been asked, "If you were given just one wish, what would that wish be?" It's a daunting question to most people; endless possibilities run through the mind contemplating things that would otherwise be unobtainable or impossible to achieve.

For a cook who comes from a family deeply rooted in its Phoenician ancestry, who has married into a Lebanese family that lives and breathes food and humble hospitality, the ultimate wish I could ever be granted would be to explore and celebrate the food traditions of the Middle East. In 2013, I was given the opportunity to create a television cooking show, *Spice Journey*, with the Australian television station Special Broadcasting Service (SBS), and travel across the Middle East, meeting cooks from all walks of life, discovering ancient and modern dishes, and then returned home to reinterpret them at my Melbourne restaurant, Maha. Three seasons on, seeing what I have seen, my spice journey has given me more than I could have ever wished for.

This book is the culmination of my travels. I'm not a natural TV show host or a travel guide. I'm not a celebrity chef or wanting to be. I'm just a cook who loves his life and all that it encompasses. My journey has taken me through the ancient lands of Persia, the Ottoman Empire, Phoenicia, the Moors, and the coastal paradise of Andalusia. I have met people who have opened their homes to me and shared their cuisine, history, and culture; but above all they have shared with me a piece of their hearts and their lives. I hope I have been able to do justice to the people who have given me so much. I hope I have portrayed their homelands in a manner that they are proud of. And I hope that I have created food that is respectful to the history and love in each special dish or item of produce that they shared.

I hope you enjoy the food and cultures I have visited during my spice journey. The recipes are all rock solid and tasty. A few have already become staples among my family and friends, and I hope the same will happen in your home soon. Cook with this book, use it, dirty it up, and put these recipes to the test. Food is something that unites people through a common ground. It is the medium for conversation and gives people a voice irrespective of race, religion, sex, or nationality.

Make these recipes your own, add your own words, and give it your own accent. People have been doing just that for centuries; that's what makes food special and why I love being a cook.

Saha!
SHANE DELIA

MALTA

Our Lady of Mount Carmel Church, St Julian's Bay

This was where it all started for me as a cook—the home of my ancestors and the place where the penny finally dropped and I decided that I was going to dedicate the rest of my life to hospitality.

The Delia family motto is *Fortis et Hospitalis,* which means "strength through hospitality." I have it tattooed on my arm and the older I get, the more I understand what it really means.

My family's homeland of Malta is a deeply misunderstood little rock. The rest of the world doesn't know what to make of it. Situated in the middle of the Mediterranean Sea, people think we are Italian, though we speak a language that has all the bones of Arabic and 95 percent of us are Roman Catholic. Over the centuries we have been invaded by nearly everyone wanting a piece of the European pie. And yet we seem to endure.

I grew up in a large Maltese family. Tales of "back home" conjured a magical place where the summers were long and hot, adventure was around every corner, and happiness awaited with every plate of food. As much as my dad was "Australian," he was always Maltese—I mean, it is hard to disguise. Our family has dark skin, Arabic features, and, no matter how hard you try, you can never quite shake off that very distinctive Maltese accent. I always wanted to get to know what made my dad the amazing person he was and finally, when I was 14, I was given that chance. Dad decided to take the whole family on a three-month vacation to Malta, to experience firsthand the country he grew up in.

We walked the same streets he did as a child, swam in the same waters, cooked and ate the same food with our family and friends, and drank in the same bars he did as a young man. We were thrown into a big, boisterous life that was not really ours, yet we were made to feel like we belonged. I immediately felt a very real connection to my ancestral home. All the stories of my father's youth came rushing in as if they were my own memories—tales from my grandparents about happy times eating and drinking, celebrating festive days by the jewel-blue Mediterranean Sea.

Malta is a deeply misunderstood little rock.
The rest of the world doesn't know what to make of it.

GOZO

N

1 2 3 4 5 6 7 8
Kilometres

MALTA

Mosta

Valletta

Paola

Żejtun

Marsaxlokk

MEDITERRANEAN

SEA

As a kid, I was under a lot of pressure to choose what I wanted to do with my life. It felt like an impossible decision. I knew that staying in school and pursuing a higher education was not really my calling, but I also knew that I needed something that not only challenged my intellect, but also stirred my soul—something through which I could connect with other people. So whether Dad knew it or not, our trip to Malta turned out to be the perfect opportunity to open my mind, my eyes, and my heart to what my soul needed.

I was immersed into a slower world: simpler, quieter, and clearer. I got the chance to listen to the sounds of day-to-day village life, rather than a busy suburb—to hear people talk and laugh, to watch the elders gossiping and berating the young, to stroll the streets taking it all in. And gradually, I realized that it was food that was binding us all together—from the packed lunch we would prepare in the morning to take with us on the long trek to our local limestone beach, to the dinner my family prepared with produce grown or reared by their own hands.

According to Maltese lore, the baker had always been the unofficial village mayor and our family had held that role for generations. Hospitality is in my blood, I realized. It is something I can neither hide nor deny. I was destined to walk the path of my ancestors, but it took coming home to this little island to hear their voice and acknowledge my path.

These days Malta has a very calming effect on me. It can be full of noise, laughter, and celebration one minute, and then so quiet the next that you can hear your own heartbeat. I love knowing that these ancient towns have seen some amazing things, and feel soothed by my father's hometown, Zejtun. I love the hole-in-the-wall vendors who sell pastizzi and the tiny bars scattered throughout the city that serve an array of little mezze to snack on while you sip beautiful Maltese wines or beer; the nannas cooking bagilla and sweet m'quaret in their kitchens, anticipating the next visit of their grandchildren; and the weathered fishermen fixing their nets in the port of Marsaxlokk, where every fishing boat has a Phoenician eye painted on its bow. I adore the carob, olives, dates, figs, spices, and oranges that fill the terraced fields of Gozo and that are an integral part of our cuisine. All of it linking us back through the ancient Phoenician bloodline that the Maltese people share. ✖

I love the hole-in-the-wall vendors who sell pastizzi and the tiny bars scattered throughout the city that serve an array of little mezze.

PORK AND PEA PASTIZZI WITH MUSTARD MAYONNAISE

I have been eating pastizzi my whole life. To say I love them is a HUGE understatement. But, while I may be a chef with Maltese heritage, I have to admit I'm probably the world's worst pastizzi maker, and when I cooked them on my spice journey it was my first real attempt. What I discovered, though, like with most things, with a little practice and patience, you will get them right.

I'm a simple guy who has always stuck to the classic ricotta filling, but every now and then, when I know the spicing is right and I'm in the mood, I'll venture over to the other side and snack on a few pea pastizzi. So this recipe is me pushing the boundaries a little with this classic, and I love the way it's turned out. The pork and pea mixture has a great taste and texture, and the introduction of the mustard mayo is the bomb!

Pastizzi freeze really well. This recipe makes a large quantity, but since the process is a bit tricky, it's a good idea to make a large batch, so set aside enough time and get some helpers.

PORK AND PEA FILLING

Combine the spices, brown sugar, soy sauce, fish sauce, and garlic in a mortar and pestle to make a paste. Rub the pork shoulder with the paste, then cover and place in the fridge overnight if you can.

Preheat the oven to 315°F (160°C).

Place the pork in a heatproof casserole dish or Dutch oven, cover with water, cover the dish with foil, and slowly cook in the oven for 4–6 hours or until the pork is tender and falling apart. Remove the pork from the dish and set aside to cool. Place the dish over high heat, bring the braising liquid to a boil, then reduce the heat to medium and simmer for 20 minutes until you have a thick sauce.

When the pork is cool enough to handle, shred the meat and pull it apart. Add to the thickened sauce, along with the peas. Mix in the chopped mint, dried mint, and almonds, and set aside.

PASTIZZI DOUGH

To make the pastizzi dough in an electric mixer, fit the mixer with the dough hook and mix the flour, salt, and 3 cups (750 ml) of water at a moderate speed for 6–8 minutes, until the dough is smooth and comes away cleanly from the sides

Pork and pea filling

3 star anise

2 cinnamon sticks

10 cloves

2½ tablespoons sabaht baharat (Lebanese 7 spice)

¼ cup (1¾ oz/50 g) light brown sugar

1 cup (250 ml) soy sauce

¼ cup (60 ml) fish sauce

2 small garlic cloves, crushed

2 lb 4 oz (1 kg) pork shoulder

generous 2 cups (12 oz/350 g) blanched or frozen peas

1 large handful mint, picked and leaves finely chopped

¼ cup (¼ oz/7 g) dried mint

2¼ cups (9 oz/250 g) slivered almonds

Pastizzi dough

8 cups (2 lb 4 oz/1 kg) all-purpose flour, plus extra for dusting

1¾ oz (50 g) salt flakes (about 6 tablespoons, depending on brand)

2 sticks plus 5 tablespoons (10½ oz/300 g) butter, at room temperature

Mustard mayonnaise

1⅓ cups (10½ oz/300 g) mayonnaise

2½ tablespoons dijon mustard

heaped tablespoon honey

of the bowl. Cover the bowl with a dish towel and leave to rest for 30 minutes. Alternatively, this dough can be mixed by hand. It will take about 20 minutes.

Once the dough has rested, sprinkle some flour on your work surface and flatten the dough with a rolling pin until it is just under ¼ inch (5mm) thick, then smear liberally with some of the softened butter. Roll the dough into a log about 4 inches (10 cm) thick, and then wrap into a coil shape. Cover in plastic wrap and refrigerate for 2 hours or until firm.

Remove the dough from the fridge and allow to soften a little. Cut the coil into quarters. Stretch each piece of dough into a long rectangle. Smear softened butter over the surface of each piece, roll each piece into a log 4 inches (10 cm) thick, then cut into ten portions roughly 1 inch (2.5 cm) thick to make 40 portions.

To make the pastizzi, flatten a pastry portion out and hold it over your thumb and index finger. Insert a tablespoon of pork and pea filling, then, in one swift motion, fold over the filling to encase it, and then flip back the other way and pinch the edges (see photo overleaf). Repeat this process until the filling and pastry are finished.

Preheat the oven to 400°F (200°C). Line three large baking trays with parchment paper.

Place the pastizzi on the prepared trays and cook for 6–8 minutes until golden.

MUSTARD MAYONNAISE

Combine the ingredients in a mixing bowl. Cover and refrigerate until required.

TO SERVE

Serve the pastizzi hot with the mustard mayonnaise.

Note It is a good idea to start this recipe one day ahead.

Pork and pea pastizzi with
mustard mayonnaise

REBECCA.

RABBIT STEW WITH RAISIN GREMOLATA

For me, no one cooked this dish, called Stuffat tal-fenek in Maltese, better than my nannu Nenu. I grew up with him making me this dish for Sunday lunches at his house. His influence on my life and my cooking has been the foundation I have built my world on. So when I was traveling in Gozo and met Joe at Ta Mena and he said he was going to cook me fenek, I was a bit worried. No way his version could be better then Nannu's!

To be honest, I wasn't expecting much when I sat down to try the dish, but that's where it all changed. The first mouthful I tasted was amazing—sweet, spice tones, thick sauce, and tender juicy rabbit. I was blown away, and I couldn't wipe the smile off my face. But even though it was beautiful, you can't get me to say it was better than Nannu's. I can say, though, that the next time I go to Gozo I'll be knocking on Joe's door and expecting a bowl of this wonderful rabbit stew.

1 whole white farmed rabbit
    (about 1 lb 12 oz/800 g)
¼ cup (60 ml) olive oil
2 cinnamon sticks
¼ teaspoon ground cloves
1 teaspoon ground turmeric
½ teaspoon ground cumin
½ teaspoon ground coriander
2 yellow onions, diced
¼ cup (1¾ oz/50 g) light brown sugar
1 teaspoon salt flakes
1 teaspoon malt vinegar
¼ cup (2¼ oz/60 g) tomato paste
3 cups (750 ml) dry red wine

Raisin gremolata
1 baguette
2½ tablespoons ghee (clarified
    butter), melted
generous ½ cup (2¾ oz/80 g) pine
    nuts, toasted
¾ cup (3½ oz/100 g) golden raisins
small handful Italian parsley, leaves
    picked
zest of 2 lemons

Break the rabbit into large chunks or ask your butcher to do this for you. Season with salt and freshly ground black pepper.

Heat 2 tablespoons of the olive oil in a Dutch oven over high heat. Add the rabbit pieces and cook for a few minutes on each side until evenly browned. Remove the meat and set aside. Add the spices, onion, sugar, salt, and malt vinegar to the pot and cook for a few minutes until the onion has softened. Add the tomato paste and stir through, then return the rabbit to the pot, add the wine, and cook for about 15 minutes until the sauce has thickened.

Add enough water to cover the rabbit, place a lid on top, and simmer for about 1½ hours or until the meat comes away from the bone. Remove the rabbit from the pot, gently pull the meat away from the bones, and discard the bones.

Meanwhile, preheat the oven to 350°F (180°C).

To make the raisin gremolata, put the baguette in a food processor and blend into coarse crumbs. Transfer the crumbs onto a baking tray and pour in the ghee, coating the crumbs evenly. Bake for 8 minutes or until golden brown. Remove from the oven and, while still hot, mix in the pine nuts, raisins, parsley, and lemon zest.

Divide the rabbit between six serving bowls and top with the sauce. Drizzle with the remaining oil, sprinkle with the raisin gremolata, and serve.

The fishing port, Marsaxlokk

Mohammad Al-Amin Mosque, Beirut

LEBANON

I thought I was prepared for what Lebanon was going to show me, but once I became immersed I quickly realized that this place was going to be so much more than I'd ever imagined.

L ebanon is special to me for more than just food. Maha, my wife, is of Lebanese descent, and the region is also the place where my Phoenician ancestors set sail into the Mediterranean, taking food, wine, and art to the rest of the world.

The food culture of Lebanon is about more than just a meal—it is part of the national identity, a reason for living. When winter draws to an end, so comes the most important season in the Lebanese kitchen... Spring brings new life and the country celebrates its diverse regional crops. The rush is on to capture its beauty and freshness, to harvest those flavors for the months ahead. Fruit is preserved, orange blossoms and rose petals distilled, herbs and spices dried, vegetables pickled, wheat and yogurt fermented, and spring lamb is slow cooked in its own fat. All of which create the intricate and diverse base to Lebanon's cuisine.

But what really took me by surprise on my culinary journey to Lebanon and put a huge smile on my face was the overwhelming hospitality of the people and their live-for-today mentality. People opened their homes and welcomed me as family. Their generosity of spirit to give without expectation touched me deeply, and the pride and happiness I witnessed when people shared prized family recipes was truly overwhelming.

Beirut itself is like no other city I have ever been to. One moment you are walking past an ancient monument, almost inhaling its presence and imagining what things would have been like thousands of years ago, the next you look to your left and see the shelled-out buildings that serve as a constant reminder of the stress and uncertainty that colors the recent past.

Lebanon is a contradiction on so many levels, but it all adds to the charm and beauty of the place. It has a sturdy soul that seems capable of getting through anything and is ever-present no matter where you go. From the snow-capped mountains, through the produce-rich Bekaa Valley, along the sun-kissed coast, to the rock-star-studded beauty of the Corniche promenade in Beirut, Lebanon excites me and has drawn me in. ✖

The food culture of Lebanon is about more than just a meal— it is a part of the national identity, a reason for living.

ARAK-CURED KINGFISH WITH SMASHED RADISH DRESSING

I was so amazed with the quality and the variety of the seafood on offer in Lebanon—so fresh—and the atmosphere in the Tripoli fish markets really got my heart pumping. This dish pays tribute to the fresh vibrant seafood that is one of the real hidden gems of Lebanon.

Mix all the kingfish curing ingredients together in a bowl.

Place the kingfish on a tray and cover with the curing mixture. Cover with plastic wrap and refrigerate for 5 hours to cure (see note).

Meanwhile, to make the smashed radish dressing, mix all the ingredients, except the radishes, together in a bowl. Smash the radishes with the underside of a heavy-based saucepan. Add the radishes to the bowl and toss to coat.

Shake the salt mixture from the kingfish and rinse off any excess. Pat dry with paper towels and then slice into ¼ inch (5 mm) slices.

Arrange the sliced kingfish on each serving plate. Add small dollops of mayonnaise, top with the radish, spoon over any remaining dressing, scatter with the arugula, if using, and serve.

Note It is important to remove the fish from the cure after 5 hours to stop the curing process.

Arak-cured kingfish

9 oz (250 g) kosher salt (about 1 cup, depending on brand)

1¼ cups (9 oz/250 g) sugar

5 star anise

10 thyme sprigs

½ cup (120 ml) Lebanese arak (or ouzo or Pernod)

small handful thyme leaves

1 side sashimi-grade kingfish (about 3 lb 5 oz/1.5 kg), skin removed

Smashed radish dressing

1 preserved lemon, peel only, finely diced

2 French shallots, finely diced

1 teaspoon Aleppo pepper*

1 tablespoon orange blossom water*

2½ tablespoons olive oil

6 French breakfast radishes (or other radishes)

¼ cup (60 ml) Kewpie mayonnaise, to serve

arugula leaves, to serve (optional)

GRILLED HALOUMI WITH POMEGRANATE AND SUMAC DRESSING

Simplicity and freshness, for me, are the two things any good cuisine is built on.

This dish is one you see throughout Lebanon. I remember driving from Beirut to Sidon and stopping on the side of the road at a simple store where a man with a huge moustache was making fresh cheese sandwiches—one man, a toaster, some labneh, haloumi, a mound of fresh flatbread, spices, olive oil, and a few other bits and pieces. He had a line out of the door!

This man cooked me a toasted sandwich with haloumi and za'atar drizzled with olive oil and local sea salt. I sat on the curb outside of his shop and savored every mouthful. Simple, fresh, and cooked with love. Heaven.

Combine all the ingredients, except the haloumi, in a mixing bowl. Check for seasoning and adjust if necessary.

Heat a large grill pan or frying pan over high heat. Add the haloumi and cook for 1 minute on each side or until golden. Press the haloumi with a spatula; when there is no resistance, the haloumi is cooked. Remove the haloumi from the pan and transfer onto paper towels to drain, then divide among serving plates. Drizzle with the pomegranate and sumac dressing and serve immediately.

1 teaspoon pumpkin seeds, toasted
seeds from 1 small pomegranate
heaped 1 tablespoon pomegranate molasses*
1 teaspoon za'atar* (or dried thyme)
1 cocktail onion, finely diced
1 teaspoon pine nuts, toasted
heaped 1 tablespoon sumac*
a few rosemary sprigs
⅔ cup (150 ml) olive oil
pinch of salt flakes
10½ oz (300 g) haloumi cheese, sliced into ½ inch (1 cm) thick portions

SHELLFISH MOGHRABIEH

Tripoli is one of those places that has little secrets around every corner.
I found so many beautiful dishes while visiting there—fish, sweets, killer
hummus—and in the winding alleys of the ancient souk I stumbled across
traditional handmade moghrabieh (large couscous).

A great technique I picked up is to boil a whole peeled onion in a
saucepan of water to soften it, then dice it and fold it through the fresh
cinnamon-spiced couscous. It gives the onion a really soft and sweet
texture, but still keeps it crisp and sharp—a real surprise and point of
difference in such a simple street-food dish.

Cook the onion in a saucepan of lightly salted boiling water over medium–high
heat for 15 minutes, then remove with a slotted spoon and set aside to cool. Add
the moghrabieh to the pan and cook for 10–12 minutes or until softened. Drain
and set aside. Chop the onion.

Heat the olive oil and butter in a frying pan over high heat, then add the
shrimp and scallops and cook for a few minutes, until just opaque. Add the
moghrabieh to the pan, along with the chopped onion, chickpeas, cinnamon,
and thyme. Toss to combine, then cook for 2 minutes to warm through. Remove
from the heat, add the lemon juice, and season with salt.

Place the shellfish moghrabieh into bowls and scatter with the shaved
vegetables and mint. Serve immediately.

1 yellow onion, peeled
1¾ cups (12 oz/350 g) moghrabieh
 (or pearl couscous)
1 tablespoon olive oil
1 tablespoon (½ oz/15 g) butter
12 raw shrimp, peeled and deveined,
 tails left intact
12 scallops
¾ cup (4¼ oz/120 g) cooked or
 canned chickpeas, rinsed and
 drained
2½ tablespoons ground cinnamon
handful chopped thyme
2½ tablespoons lemon juice
2 French breakfast radishes (or other
 radishes), thinly shaved
2 baby turnips, thinly shaved
small handful mint leaves, to serve

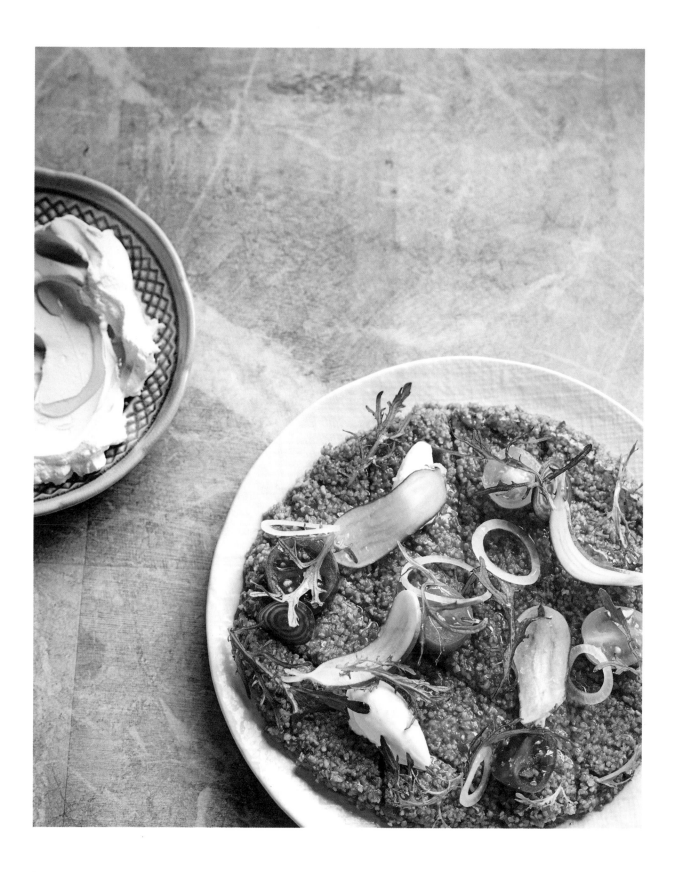

CRACKED WHEAT AND TOMATO KIBBEH

Talk about my idea of heaven ... Sitting on the beach with my feet in the sand listening to the sounds of Lebanese pop music drifting through the air, watching children play in the water, an ice-cold Lebanese beer in one hand and eating simply cooked line-caught fish with this beautiful vegetarian tomato kibbeh. I don't know how you could top it.

Soak the bulgur in a bowl of hot tap water for 30 minutes or until soft. Drain.

Using a food processor, grind the bulgur, tomato, and onion into an even consistency. Alternatively, use a grinder. Transfer the bulgur mixture to a bowl and add the remaining ingredients, tasting as you go to balance the flavors; if one flavor dominates, adjust by adding more of the other ingredients. Cover with plastic wrap and refrigerate until required.

Place the radish, beet, onion, and arugula into separate bowls of iced water and leave to crisp for about 10 minutes. Drain on paper towels.

Arrange the bulgur mixture on a serving plate and add a few dollops of yogurt. Top with the thinly sliced vegetables, arugula, and tomatoes. Drizzle with olive oil and serve immediately.

Kibbeh

1½ cups (9¼ oz/265 g) fine bulgur
1 large tomato
½ red onion
heaped 1 tablespoon dried mint
heaped 1 tablespoon sumac*
1 teaspoon smoked paprika
pinch of cayenne pepper
heaped 1 tablespoon red pepper paste*
2½ tablespoons pomegranate molasses*
10 mint leaves, finely chopped
10 cilantro leaves, finely chopped
drizzle of olive oil

1 radish, thinly sliced
1 candy beet (or another heirloom beet), thinly sliced
1 cocktail onion, thinly sliced
handful arugula leaves
¼ cup (2¼ oz/60 g) Greek yogurt
handful small heirloom tomatoes, halved
drizzle of extra virgin olive oil

The coast near Anfeh

LAMB AND KISHK KIBBEH

I am crazy about sour flavors, and in today's cooking we in the West all seem to be getting excited about preservation and fermentation in food.

I remember watching women laying out freshly made kishk paste on cheesecloth on a rooftop in the Lebanese foothills so it could ferment and dry under the warm Lebanese sun—in the Middle East this kind of stuff has been going on since time began.

To make the casing, soak the bulgur in a bowl of hot tap water for 30 minutes or until soft. Drain well; you don't want excess moisture in this casing.

Tip the bulgur into a food processor and add the sabaht baharat, salt, and lamb, and combine well. Transfer into a bowl, cover with plastic wrap, and refrigerate until required.

Next, make the kishk farce filling. Bring a saucepan of water to a boil over medium–high heat. Score the bases of the tomatoes, then blanch them for 10 seconds. Refresh the tomatoes in iced water, then peel off the skins and discard. Quarter the tomatoes, remove the seeds, and cut them into ½ inch (1 cm) cubes.

Combine the tomatoes and remaining ingredients in a bowl, and mix together to a sticky consistency. Season to taste.

To make the kibbeh, put an egg-sized amount of the casing mixture in your hand and form it into a ball. Poke a hole in the ball with your finger and then make a space for the filling with a tablespoon. Add a teaspoon of the filling and pinch the top to seal the ball. Repeat with the remaining casing and filling mixtures to make about 30 kibbeh.

Pour some canola oil into a deep frying pan to a depth of about 1½ inches (4 cm), then heat over medium–high heat until it shimmers. If you have a kitchen thermometer, the oil will be ready when the temperature reaches 350°F (180°C). Alternatively, use a deep-fryer.

Carefully add the kibbeh to the pan in batches and cook for 3–5 minutes or until golden brown. Drain on paper towels, then serve with some yogurt.

Note Kishk powder is made from fermented bulgur and yogurt, which is then dried and ground into a powder. It is available at specialist Middle Eastern grocery stores and online.

1⅔ cups (10½ oz/300 g) fine bulgur
1 teaspoon sabaht baharat*
(Lebanese 7 spice)
pinch of salt flakes
13 oz (360 g) lean ground lamb leg
canola oil, for deep-frying

Kishk farce filling

4 oxheart tomatoes (or another large heirloom tomatoes)
½ yellow onion, finely diced
4 Swiss chard stalks, leaves finely chopped
1 cup (5½ oz/150 g) cooked or canned chickpeas, rinsed, drained, and smashed
1 cup (3½ oz/100 g) kishk powder (see note)
¼ cup (2¼ oz/60 g) Greek yogurt, plus extra to serve
2½ tablespoons dried mint
drizzle of olive oil

STUFFED CHICKEN WINGS WITH SOUR CHERRY BARBECUE SAUCE

Street food in Beirut is a big deal. Hundreds of hole-in-the-wall vendors and street-side food sellers all produce killer cheap bites that are hard to beat. This is a dish that pays homage to the Armenian community in Beirut who cook skillfully flavored street-food dishes using sweet and sour tones, all balanced out with heat and spice.

Remove the casings from the sucuk sausages. Fill the cavities of the chicken wings with about 1 tablespoon of the sucuk.

Bring a saucepan of water to a boil over medium–high heat. Place half of the chicken wings in a bamboo steamer with at least ½ inch (1 cm) gap between them and place the steamer on top of the pan. Steam for 10–15 minutes—the steaming process will cause the cooked chicken meat to plump up a little. To check if they are cooked properly, you can use a skewer. Push the skewer through the middle and leave for 10 seconds; when it comes out, it should feel "body temperature," i.e. not cold on the fingertips. Transfer the stuffed chicken wings to a plate and repeat with the remaining stuffed chicken wings. Cover the plate with plastic wrap and refrigerate until fully cold.

Combine the flour, garlic powder, onion powder, sweet paprika, cayenne pepper, salt, black pepper, tomato soup powder, rice flour, and cornflakes in a large bowl. Mix evenly. Set aside until required.

To make the sour cherry barbecue sauce, combine all of the sauce ingredients, except the puréed sour cherries, with 1 cup (250 ml) of water in a saucepan and place over medium–high heat. Bring to a boil, then reduce to a simmer and cook, uncovered, stirring frequently, for 40 minutes. Remove the saucepan from the heat and add the puréed sour cherries. Set aside to cool.

Put the buttermilk in a bowl. Remove the chicken wings from the fridge and, one at a time, place them into the buttermilk to lightly coat, then transfer to the flour mixture and roll around to evenly coat. Place on a tray and repeat the process until all the chicken wings are coated.

Pour some canola oil into a deep frying pan, until about 1½ inches (4 cm) deep, then heat over medium–high heat until it shimmers. If you have a kitchen thermometer, the oil will be ready when the temperature reaches 350°F (180°C). Alternatively, use a deep-fryer.

Carefully add the chicken wings to the pan, a few at a time, and deep fry for 3–4 minutes, until golden brown. Drain on paper towels.

Serve immediately with the sour cherry barbecue sauce.

1 lb 2 oz (500 g) sucuk sausages*
16 boneless chicken wings (mid-section only—about 2¼ oz/60 g each)
4 cups (1 lb 2 oz/500 g) all-purpose flour
3 tablespoons garlic powder
3 tablespoons onion powder
2 tablespoons sweet paprika
2 tablespoons cayenne pepper
2½ tablespoons salt flakes
1 teaspoon freshly ground black pepper
½ cup (2¾ oz/80 g) instant tomato soup powder
⅔ cup (3½ oz/100 g) rice flour
3½ cups (3½ oz/100 g) cornflakes, coarsely crushed
2½ cups (600 ml) buttermilk
canola oil, for deep-frying

Sour cherry barbecue sauce

2 cups (500 ml) ketchup
1 cup (250 ml) apple cider vinegar
⅓ cup (2½ oz/70 g) light brown sugar
⅓ cup (2½ oz/70 g) sugar
2 teaspoons freshly ground black pepper
2 teaspoons onion powder
2 teaspoons mustard powder
heaped 1 tablespoon lemon juice
heaped 1 tablespoon worcestershire sauce
1¾ cups (400 ml) sour cherry juice
10½ oz (300 g) pitted sour cherries, puréed

SPICY DAHLIA FRIES

Every now and then, I meet people who really leave their mark on me. It's not always their cooking skills that stay with me; sometimes it can just be a personal connection. This was the case with a young woman punching above her weight in a male-dominated culture and industry. Dahlia ran a little pop-up fish restaurant right on the beach in the town of Tyre, called Cloud 59. Her power, confidence, attitude, and swagger made me smile.

Give these fries a try. The recipe uses frozen French fries as a starting point, so it is super simple, and the use of chili and spices really ramps up an old classic. I guarantee the hardest part will be stopping yourself from making a second batch straight away. Thanks Dahlia!

Pour some canola oil into a deep frying pan to a depth of about 1½ inches (4 cm), then heat over medium–high heat until it shimmers. If you have a kitchen thermometer, the oil will be ready when the temperature reaches 350°F (180°C). Alternatively, use a deep-fryer. Carefully add the French fries to the pan and cook for 3–5 minutes until golden brown.

Meanwhile, heat the butter in a small saucepan over medium heat for 5 minutes or until nut brown in color and frothy. Remove from the heat and set aside.

Heat the olive oil in a large frying pan over medium–high heat, add the garlic, and sauté until soft and fragrant. Add the fries, straight from the pan, then add the almonds, Aleppo pepper, sumac, and ground coriander. Toss really well to ensure all the seasonings are well dispersed. Drizzle with the brown butter and scatter with the cilantro leaves. Place in a serving dish with lemon wedges on the side and serve immediately.

Note Spicy Dahlia fries are great served on their own, but are also delicious served with grilled fish and at barbecues.

canola oil, for deep-frying
1 lb 2 oz (500 g) frozen crinkle-cut French fries
1 stick (4 oz/115 g) butter
2½ tablespoons olive oil
2 garlic cloves, crushed
½ cup (1¾ oz/50 g) sliced almonds, toasted
pinch of Aleppo pepper*
pinch of sumac*
pinch of ground coriander
cilantro leaves, to serve
lemon wedges, to serve

DUCK AWARMA

Awarma is not only a really tasty ingredient, but it is a way for people to preserve meat for years on end with no refrigeration. I wanted to take this same technique and introduce a little more spice, using duck instead of the traditional lamb, and I'm really happy with the result.

Once you have this on hand, you can serve it with hummus and flatbread (see page 53), stirred through risotto (see page 54), or as part of a Middle Eastern banquet.

Place the duck in a bowl and completely cover with the salt. Leave to rest for 30 minutes, then rinse off and pat dry with paper towels.

Heat a heavy-based saucepan over high heat. Add the duck meat and cook, stirring frequently, for about 15 minutes until the fat has rendered down and the meat is caramelized. Add the spices and caramelize for another couple of minutes. Reduce the heat to very low, add the duck fat, and cook for at least 2 hours. Remove from the heat, transfer to a large sterilized jar and store in the refrigerator.

Notes Duck fat is available from select supermarkets and poultry suppliers. Look for jars or tins. Like other fats, it is solid at room temperature, but melts quickly with heat.

Add additional spices to the jar, if you like, such as star anise, cloves, and black peppercorns.

2 x 6½ oz (180 g) duck breasts, skin and sinews removed, diced

1 lb 2 oz (500 g) kosher salt (about 1½ cups, depending on brand)

¼ cup (1 oz/30 g) sabaht baharat* (Lebanese 7 spice)

4 cardamom pods

2 bay leaves

2 cinnamon sticks

1 lb 2 oz (500 g) duck fat (see note)

HUMMUS WITH DUCK AWARMA AND CUMIN FLATBREAD

I loved the time I got to spend with the Druze community in Lebanon, learning their food history—awarma is one of their traditional preserving techniques. This dish combines the sweet notes of duck awarma with the creaminess of hummus, and is served with freshly made cumin flatbread to mop it all up and make a delicious feast of flavor.

HUMMUS

Put the chickpeas in a food processor and blend until smooth—you may need to frequently scrape down the sides to begin with. Add the remaining ingredients and gradually pour in a scant 1 cup (200 ml) hot tap water, blending to a smooth purée. Taste and adjust the seasoning if necessary. Refrigerate until required.

CUMIN FLATBREAD

Using an electric stand mixer with the dough hook attachment, combine the flour, salt, yogurt, cumin seeds, garlic, and ½ cup (120 ml) lukewarm water at a moderate speed for 5–7 minutes, until the dough is smooth and comes away cleanly from the side of the bowl. Be careful not to overwork or it will become tough. Cover the bowl with a dish towel and leave to rest in a warm place for 30 minutes to double in size. Divide into six, roll into balls, and allow to proof on a baking tray, covered, for about 20 minutes.

Sprinkle some flour on your work surface and flatten the dough with a rolling pin to ¹⁄₁₆ inch (2 mm) thick. Leave to proof again for 10 minutes.

Heat a frying pan or grill pan over high heat. Lightly brush with olive oil and add the flatbreads, one at a time, and cook for about 2 minutes on each side until crisp and browned. Keep warm.

TO ASSEMBLE

Heat a frying pan over high heat. Add the duck awarma and the nuts. Cook for 4–5 minutes, stirring frequently to allow the nuts to evenly color and the duck to warm through. Add the baby figs, cook for another 30 seconds, and stir until well combined.

Spoon the hummus into the center of a serving dish, make a well in the middle, and pour in the duck mixture. Place the cumin flatbreads on the side and serve immediately.

Hummus
scant 2 cups (10½ oz/300 g) cooked or canned chickpeas, rinsed and drained
6 tablespoons (3½ oz/100 g) tahini*
2 garlic cloves
⅔ cup (150 ml) lemon juice
2 tablespoons salt flakes
3 tablespoons olive oil

Cumin flatbread
2⅓ cups (10½ oz/300 g) all-purpose flour, plus extra for dusting
1 teaspoon salt flakes
¼ cup (2¼ oz/60 g) Greek yogurt
1 teaspoon toasted and coarsely crushed cumin seeds
2 garlic cloves, pounded
olive oil, for frying

To assemble
1 quantity duck awarma (see page 50)
⅓ cup (1¾ oz/50 g) pine nuts
⅓ cup (1¾ oz/50 g) blanched almonds
1 cup (5½ oz/150 g) dried baby figs, soaked (or fresh figs if in season)

FREEKEH RISOTTO WITH DUCK AWARMA, POACHED EGGS, AND TOASTED NUTS

This is one dish in Lebanon that I can honestly say really took my breath away. Simple but complex flavor all brought together by that amazing grain, freekeh. So beautiful.

The Bekaa Valley is the food center of Lebanon—its nutrient-rich soil gives life to everything that it produces. So when I had the chance to drink wine from the ancient Phoenician region that gave birth to all viticulture around the world, and eat this simple humble dish sourced from local fields, how could I say no?

Soak the freekeh in a bowl of water overnight. Drain.

Bring the chicken stock to a boil in a saucepan over medium–high heat.

Heat the olive oil in a frying pan over medium–low heat, add the onions, and cook for about 5 minutes to caramelize. Add the wine and allow to reduce by half, then add the drained freekeh and stir through. Add a ladleful of stock and stir until it has been absorbed, then continue to cook, adding the stock, a ladleful at a time, for 25–30 minutes until all the stock has been added and the freekeh has the appearance of risotto.

Meanwhile, place a wide-based saucepan over high heat, add the duck awarma and some of the duck fat from the jar, the nuts, cinnamon, bay leaf, and sabaht baharat, and gently cook until golden. Remove from the heat and set aside.

Sprinkle the chopped herbs and arugula into the risotto, fold in the butter, season, and divide between each serving dish. Spoon the duck and nut mixture on top. Using the back of a spoon, make indentations in the mixture for the eggs. Carefully add the eggs—being careful not to pop the yolks—and then grate some kefalograviera over the top. Serve immediately.

1¼ cups (7 oz/200 g) freekeh

4 cups (1 liter) chicken stock

2½ tablespoons olive oil

2 onions, finely diced

1 cup (250 ml) dry white wine

heaped 3 tablespoons duck awarma (see page 50)

1 cup (3½ oz/100 g) walnuts, halved

⅓ cup (1¾ oz/50 g) pine nuts

¾ cup (3½ oz/100 g) blanched almonds

1 cinnamon stick

1 bay leaf

1 teaspoon sabaht baharat* (Lebanese 7 spice)

2 handfuls Italian parsley, finely chopped

2 handfuls cilantro, leaves finely chopped

handful arugula leaves

3½ tablespoons (1¾ oz/50 g) butter, diced small

4 soft-poached eggs, to serve

3½ oz (100 g) kefalograviera cheese (or another hard sheep's cheese)

LAMB SFIHA

You can really tell a lot about a country by the quality of its street food. And if Lebanon was going to be judged this way, then these little parcels of heaven from Baalbek would get my vote!

So simple, but soooo tasty, these little mini pizzas are the type of food I really love. Great dough, really fresh ingredients, and when they are cooked right in front of you and you can sit on the side of the road and eat them—well, that's what life is all about.

Put the lamb, squash, onion, garlic, Aleppo pepper, and tomatoes in a food processor and mix until well combined. Season with salt and black pepper. Keep refrigerated until required.

In a bowl, dissolve the yeast in 1¾ cups (400 ml) of lukewarm water.

Combine the flour and salt in the bowl of an electric stand mixer and attach the dough hook. Commence mixing on a low speed and slowly add the yeast and water mixture and the olive oil. Increase the speed slightly and mix for 5–8 minutes until smooth.

Sprinkle some flour on a tray. Divide the dough into 20 balls and place on the tray, leaving plenty of space around them. Cover with a dish towel and set aside in a warm place for 20–30 minutes to double in size.

Place a pizza stone or baking tray in the oven and preheat to 400°F (200°C).

Sprinkle some flour on your work surface and, using a rolling pin, flatten the dough balls into squares about ⅛ inch (3 mm) thick. Place a large tablespoon of the lamb mixture in the middle of a square and flatten it out. Pinch together two opposite corners and repeat with the other side. You should end up with four-cornered pastry squares with the filling in the middle. Repeat until you have used all the mixture and dough.

Place the sfiha on the preheated pizza stone or baking tray and cook for about 3–5 minutes until golden. Remove from the oven, scatter with the mint leaves, and serve with lemon wedges.

1 lb 12 oz (800 g) lean ground lamb leg

7 oz (200 g) kabocha squash (or other winter squash), roughly chopped

1 red onion, roughly chopped

2 garlic cloves, roughly chopped

2½ tablespoons Aleppo pepper*

2 vine-ripened tomatoes, roughly chopped

3 envelopes (¾ oz/20 g) active dry yeast

4½ cups (1 lb 6 oz/625 g) bread flour, plus extra for dusting

2½ teaspoons salt flakes

splash of olive oil

handful mint, leaves picked

lemon wedges, to serve

RICOTTA AND CAROB LADY FINGERS

Carob is one of those ingredients that people don't really understand or don't give too much respect to. I have to admit I used to be one of those people, but after traveling through Malta and Lebanon I started to realize how beautiful carob is and how important it once was. Did you know, so the story goes, that carob seeds were originally used as the standard measure for precious stones? Over time the word corrupted, and we now have the word "carat."

Line a large bowl with cheesecloth. Place the ricotta into the cheesecloth and leave to drain, covered, in the fridge overnight.

Combine the drained ricotta, carob, and almonds in a bowl and stir well.

Place 2 tablespoons of the ricotta filling onto a piece of brik pastry and roll into a log shape, then fold in the edges. Brush the edges with the egg yolk to seal. Repeat this process until all the pastry is used, to make about 8 fingers.

Pour some canola oil into a frying pan to about 1½ inches (4 cm) deep, then heat over medium–high heat until it shimmers. If you have a kitchen thermometer, the oil will be ready when the temperature reaches 340°F (170°C). Alternatively, use a deep-fryer. Carefully add the pastries, a few at a time, and deep-fry for 3–4 minutes or until golden brown. Transfer to paper towels to drain and dust with confectioner's sugar.

Place the lady fingers on a wooden board or serving platter, garnish with some cotton candy, and serve immediately.

Notes This dish is traditionally made with areesh (a drained yogurt cheese), but ricotta is an easy replacement.

You can find carob molasses, brik pastry, and Middle Eastern cotton candy in Middle Eastern grocery stores.

¾ cup (7 oz/200 g) ricotta (see note)

⅓ cup (4 oz/115 g) carob molasses (see note)

2½ tablespoons sliced almonds, toasted

8 sheets brik pastry* (see note)

1 egg yolk

canola oil, for deep-frying

confectioner's sugar, for dusting

2¾ oz (80 g) chocolate cotton candy (pashmak) (see note)

CANDIED SPICED PUMPKIN

The preservation of fruit in the mountains of Lebanon is a celebration of life. Lebanon moves with the seasons, and when fruit and vegetables are harvested it's about enjoying them at their peak as well as preserving them for the colder months ahead.

I was really touched and inspired by the amazing women I met at Mymoune, an artisan food company and women's refuge in the Lebanese foothills. Their stories, passion, and skill really resonated with me, and opened my world to some wonderful creations.

I love this recipe because it shows the beauty of pumpkin—such a simple vegetable often overlooked as just a soup vegetable or side to be served with roast dinners.

Place the sugar, cloves, cardamom pods, vanilla beans and seeds, bay leaf, cinnamon stick, and 2½ cups (600 ml) of water in a large saucepan and bring to a boil over high heat. Reduce the heat and simmer for 5 minutes or until the sugar has dissolved. Set aside.

Cut the pumpkin in half and scrape out the seeds. Cut the flesh into thick wedges.

Bring a large saucepan of water to a boil over high heat. Add the pumpkin, reduce the heat to a simmer, and cook for 10 minutes or until the pumpkin is soft but still holds its shape. Carefully remove the pumpkin from the pan and divide between sterilized jars or clean containers. Add the orange blossom water and the spiced syrup to the jars to cover the pumpkin, allow to cool, cover with the lids, and then refrigerate for at least 24 hours so the pumpkin takes on the flavor of the syrup.

Notes Store in the fridge until use.

Serve as an accompaniment with the fig and walnut ice cream (see page 62). Use as the basis for pumpkin Turkish delight (see page 161).

3 cups (1 lb 5 oz/600 g) sugar
10 cloves
12 cardamom pods, crushed
2 vanilla beans, split and seeds scraped
1 bay leaf
1 cinnamon stick
2 lb 4 oz (1 kg) kabocha squash (or other winter squash)
scant ½ cup (100 ml) orange blossom water*

FIG AND WALNUT ICE CREAM

These flavors are the soul of the Lebanese mountains. In season, you can smell the sweet caramel aroma oozing out of the sun-ripened figs. Roasted walnuts add a special earthy contrast to the sweet honey-like goodness of the figs in this ice cream. I love this recipe and it's a great one to just sit in front of the TV with, grab a spoon, and devour. You don't need an ice cream maker to pull this one off.

To make the fig paste, put the figs and sugar in a saucepan with 2 cups (500 ml) of water over medium heat and stir until the sugar has dissolved. Bring to a boil, then reduce the heat and simmer for 30 minutes or until the figs are really soft. Place the fig mixture in a food processor and purée to make a smooth paste.

Place the sugar and 1 cup (250 ml) of water in a saucepan over low heat and stir to dissolve. Add the fig paste, remove from the heat, and use a hand-held immersion blender to purée until smooth. Set aside to cool.

Fold the walnuts through the fig mixture.

Using an electric stand mixer with the whisk attachment, beat the egg yolks at medium–high speed until thick and pale. Add to the cooled fig paste mix.

Using the electric stand mixer with the whisk attachment, whip the cream to soft peaks.

Fold the egg and fig paste mixture into the cream. Pour into a container and freeze for 2–3 hours.

Remove the fig and walnut ice cream from the freezer and leave to soften slightly. Serve with fresh figs and walnuts or with candied spiced pumpkin (see page 61).

Fig paste

3⅓ cups (1 lb 2 oz/500 g) dried white figs
2¼ cups (1 lb/450 g) sugar

¾ cup (5¾ oz/165 g) superfine sugar
2 cups (7 oz/200 g) walnuts, crushed, plus extra to serve
4 egg yolks
2 cups (500 ml) whipping cream
4 fresh ripe figs, to serve

ROAST PEANUT BUTTER PARFAIT, TAHINI SALTED CARAMEL, AND BROKEN BAKLAVA

Helleb's Sweets in Tripoli is one of the most amazing sweet shops I have ever visited. Entrenched in history and using breathtaking techniques, they produce some stellar traditional Lebanese sweets. The baklava I tried there was just incredible.

For me, a good baklava has to have crunch, a toasted buttery, nutty flavor, and hints of caramel, normally brought together by the over-the-top sweet syrup it is drenched in. I don't think you can beat the original baklava I tried at Helleb's, so I am not even going to try. This dish pays homage to all the things I love about baklava, but with a twist. It's a great dish that you can cook for friends and family, and claim as your own. It's a winner!

ROAST PEANUT BUTTER PARFAIT

Preheat the oven to 340°F (170°C).

Put the peanuts on a baking tray and roast for 8 minutes or until golden brown. Transfer into a food processor and blend until as smooth as possible. Add 1¼ cups (300 ml) of the cream and continue to blend to a thick peanut butter-like consistency. Set aside.

Whip 1⅓ cups (325 ml) of the cream to stiff peaks using an electric stand mixer with the whisk attachment and then set aside.

Combine the peanut mixture with the remaining ⅓ cup (75 ml) or so of cream in a bowl. Fold through the whipped cream. Set aside.

Place the egg yolks in the bowl of the electric mixer and whisk on high speed until pale. Reduce the speed to low and continue to whisk while you make the syrup.

Put the sugar, glucose, and 2½ tablespoons of water in a small saucepan over high heat, bring to a boil, and cook to soft ball stage—to test if the syrup is ready drop a small amount into a shallow bowl of cold water to cool it down. It should form a soft ball. If you have a kitchen thermometer, the syrup will be ready when the temperature reaches about 240°F (115–118°C).

Gradually pour the syrup into the egg yolks. Once all the syrup has been added, increase the speed and whip for 15 minutes or until cool.

Fold the egg mixture through the peanut butter cream until well combined. Pour into six serving bowls and freeze for 4 hours.

Roast peanut butter parfait

1⅓ cups (7 oz/200 g) peanuts
3 cups (750 ml) whipping cream
8 egg yolks
1¼ cups (9 oz/250 g) superfine sugar
¼ cup (60 ml) liquid glucose*

Broken baklava

12 sheets filo pastry, at room temperature
generous ¾ cup (7 oz/200 g) melted ghee (clarified butter)
⅔ cup (3½ oz/100 g) pine nuts, coarsely crushed
½ cup (1¾ oz/50 g) walnuts, coarsely crushed
¾ cup (3½ oz/100 g) blanched almonds, coarsely crushed
½ cup (2¾ oz/80 g) cinnamon sugar (see note)

Tahini salted caramel

¼ cup (60 ml) liquid glucose*
6 tablespoons (2½ oz/75 g) sugar
⅓ cup (75 ml) milk
4½ tablespoons (2¼ oz/60 g) butter
⅔ cup (150 ml) whipping cream
scant ⅔ cup (5½ oz/150 g) tahini*
pinch of salt flakes

To serve

good quality chocolate ice cream

BROKEN BAKLAVA

Lay 1 filo sheet on a baking tray and brush with a little ghee. Add a sprinkle of each of the nuts and the cinnamon sugar and then place another layer of filo on top. Brush with more ghee. Continue layering with nuts, cinnamon sugar, and filo until all the filo sheets are used, ending up with a layer of filo. Transfer to the fridge and leave for 20 minutes until it sets.

Preheat the oven to 345°F (175°C). Remove the pastry from the fridge.

Put the baklava in the oven and cook for 12 minutes or until golden. Remove from the oven, leave to cool, then break up into shards. Set aside (see note).

TAHINI SALTED CARAMEL

Combine the glucose, sugar, milk, and butter in a saucepan and simmer over medium heat for 5–10 minutes, stirring occasionally, until the mixture thickens and turns creamy caramel in color.

Meanwhile, put the cream in a separate saucepan and bring to a gentle simmer over low heat.

When the caramel is golden and has thickened, add the heated cream, tahini, and salt to the pan, and mix. Pass the mixture through a fine sieve into a bowl to remove any lumps. Set aside.

TO SERVE

Remove the roast peanut butter parfait and chocolate ice cream from the freezer and set aside to soften slightly.

Place some tahini salted caramel on top of the peanut butter parfait. Top with a scoop of chocolate ice cream, add the broken baklava, and serve.

Notes You can buy cinnamon sugar at the supermarket. You can make it, too, combining equal parts (by volume) ground cinnamon and sugar.

You can make the broken baklava ahead and store in an airtight container.

Roast peanut butter parfait,
tahini salted caramel, and
broken baklava

Golestan Palace, Tehran

Like many people around the world, all I knew about Iran was either what Western media wanted me to know, or embellished tales of the great Persian Empire in all of its opulence and glory.

What I found was something different again. Certainly, I did find a place of profound beauty and elegance steeped in historical and religious grandeur, with guardians of a cuisine that was like no other I had encountered during my journey thus far. But that's where my preconceived and rather stereotypical view of the Iranian people ended.

The food was exciting. Sweet dried and preserved fruits, sour pomegranate dishes studded with walnuts and perfumed with fragrant spices that seemed to subtly unlock the hidden flavors of the dishes, and techniques for cooking perfect rice that remain unchallenged by any other cuisine. We feasted on smoked rice dishes, sweet rice dishes, and witnessed a skill for baking an inch-thick, maddeningly crisp crust on rice called tadek, which blew me away. We refreshed ourselves with crazy frozen rice noodle desserts that can be traced back to 400 BC. Rice and noodles—essential ingredients liberally sprinkled with Iranian food magic.

Some of the best one-pot dishes I've ever tasted were in Iran—a simple technique, yet producing balanced and exciting flavor profiles that tap into all the senses. For me this type of dish not only sums up Iranian food, but it shows the skill in which flavor is layered and balanced to achieve perfection. It captured my imagination, as did perfectly cooked Iranian flatbread: darn good on its own; better piled with fresh fragrant herbs, pickles, saffron, spices, beans, meat, and nuts, all coming together in a kind of DIY platter that really did it for me. This is real food, cooked by real people. And, in a nutshell, that's what I loved about Iran.

Sadly, I had very few great "restaurant" experiences in Iran; it seemed to me that all the best cooking was done behind closed doors, in people's homes with their families. To be honest, that is the story of most of the places I travel to, but here the divide between what you enjoy at home and what was on offer in a restaurant seemed particularly wide.

Some people may look at Middle Eastern food and say it is all the same, which is like saying all Asian food is the same. Iranian food is not Arab—it is Persian and it is

as diverse, exciting, and challenging as any other of the great cuisines of the world. Traveling through this huge country, I found food cultures that really reflected their surroundings. In the Persian Gulf there was a true Pakistani–Emirati feel to the food: exotic seafood combined with sour notes from tamarind and a little more heat than in other parts of Iran; and almost curry-style dishes that I absolutely loved, completed with the subtle refinement of Persian elegance.

Intricate and artistic spicing and cooking techniques in Shiraz not only pushed Iranian food to another level among its Middle Eastern neighbors, but also somehow embodied the graceful and laid-back nature of the city's people. There is definitely something in the air in this town, with its calming and picturesque vistas that all seemed to reflect the poetry of the great Persian poet Hafez, who called this city home.

In Esfahan and Yazd, breathtaking architecture and Islamic grandeur are reflected in the palaces and mosques, and ancient Persian romance is told through stories woven into silk rugs and paintings. All of it converges to captivate your imagination of this once great and all-conquering Persian Empire.

Having spent time in Iran it now strikes me as a tragedy that we in the West have pigeon-holed Iran, and cast it aside. Underneath all the bureaucracy and political unrest are beautiful people who are proud of their history, food, and country.

I am not the kind of person to take a political stand on a cause, or to publicly express an opinion about a complex situation, but I can say that the perception of the Iranian people I had when I arrived and the newfound respect, admiration, and love for both the people and the country that I came back with, has shaped my life and opened my eyes to a larger world than the one broadcast on CNN. ✶

Underneath all the bureaucracy and political unrest are beautiful people who are proud of their history, food, and country.

PICKLED EGGPLANTS WITH BLACK PEPPER AND GREEN CHILI

One of the greatest things I learned in Shiraz is that food is not just something to fill you up, enjoy, and move on—in that ancient city, cooking was entwined with the whole Shirazi and Persian culture. Food imitates art, art is influenced by the poets, and the poets are inspired by the seasons and beauty of nature. It is all one.

This dish is so simple, but when I watched it being made and saw the delicacy of the spices being added, I began to understand the subtle sweet and sour notes from the sugar and vinegar, and I fell in love with it. My interpretation tones the dish down a little from the original and softens the heat and vinegar flavors.

Combine the eggplant slices, red wine vinegar, garlic, split chilies, spices, honey, and sugar in a large saucepan. Add 8 cups (2 liters) of water, place over high heat, and bring to a boil. Reduce to a simmer and cook for 10 minutes or until the eggplant is tender but not falling apart. Remove from the heat and leave to cool to room temperature.

Transfer to a large sterilized jar, allow to cool completely, cover, and refrigerate for at least a week.

Place the pickled eggplant into a mixing bowl, add some olive oil, and toss. Put the remaining ingredients on top and serve.

Notes The pickled eggplants need a week before it can be used.

Serve as part of a mezze platter or with the slow-roasted lamb shoulder with nomads' jeweled yogurt and nigella seed bread on page 82.

2 lb 4 oz (1 kg) Lebanese (long thin) eggplants, sliced ½ inch (1 cm) thick

4 cups (1 liter) good quality red wine vinegar

6 garlic cloves, sliced

6 green chilies, split, plus 1 extra, thinly sliced

2½ tablespoons ground turmeric

2½ tablespoons ground cumin

2½ tablespoons ground coriander

generous ½ cup (7 oz/200 g) honey

1 cup (7 oz/200 g) light brown sugar

splash of olive oil

10 mint leaves

10 cilantro leaves

heaped 1 tablespoon coriander seeds

Salt Lake, Iran

QUAIL EGG KEFTA TABRIZ

What I really love about this dish is the way the chickpeas and potatoes lift the kefta and lighten the whole mixture. There are so many versions of kefta throughout the Middle East and, to be honest, most of them taste fairly similar. Only the spicing changes and their technique of cooking. This kefta from Tabriz was really different. Soft, light, moist, and the introduction of the egg in the middle and the freshness of the tarragon really made it something special.

Put the potatoes in a saucepan and cover with cold water. Cook over medium heat for about 15 minutes or until tender. Drain, then place in a bowl with the chickpeas and mash. Set aside.

Bring another saucepan of water to a boil. Add the quail eggs and cook for 2½ minutes, then remove and refresh in iced water. Very carefully peel the shells and discard. Set aside the eggs.

Combine the ground meats in a large mixing bowl. Add the mashed potato and chickpea mixture, the tarragon, turmeric, flour, and ⅓ cup (80 ml) of the saffron water. Mix very well and then divide into 16 balls.

Dampen the palm of your hand with some water and flatten one of the balls in your palm. Place a cooked and peeled quail egg inside and then fold the meat mixture over to encase the egg, rolling to seal. Repeat this process with the rest of the meat mixture and eggs. Set aside.

Put the stock, tomato paste, and remaining saffron water in a saucepan over high heat and bring to a boil. Remove from the heat.

In a wide-based saucepan, heat the olive oil over medium–high heat. Add the onion and sauté until translucent. Add the meatballs and cook for a few minutes, turning regularly, until colored evenly on all sides. Add the orzo, cover it with some of the saffron stock, and carefully stir, being careful not to break the balls. Continue adding the stock, a ladleful at a time, stirring occasionally, for 15–20 minutes or until the meat is cooked. Add the butter to the pan, remove from the heat, and stir. Check the seasoning, then serve immediately.

7 oz (200 g) potatoes, peeled and cut into even-sized pieces
14 oz (400 g) can chickpeas, rinsed and drained
16 quail eggs
1 lb 7 oz (640 g) lean ground lamb
1 lb 7 oz (640 g) lean ground chicken
small handful tarragon, chopped
1 teaspoon ground turmeric
¾ cup (3¾ oz/110 g) bread flour
2 cups (500 ml) saffron water*
8 cups (2 liters) chicken stock
2½ tablespoons tomato paste
2½ tablespoons olive oil
1 yellow onion, diced
1 cup (7 oz/200 g) dried orzo
2½ tablespoons (1¼ oz/35 g) butter

Preparation time: 30 minutes, plus 1–2 days marinating and 45 minutes proofing • Cooking time: 12 hours • Serves: 8

SLOW-ROASTED LAMB SHOULDER WITH NOMADS' JEWELED YOGURT AND NIGELLA SEED BREAD

Traveling along the windy desert road from Esfahan to the Caspian Sea was a hard and long journey—such a huge country with so much untouched countryside that it is easy to get lost in the never-ending and always changing surroundings. During a pit stop, I stumbled across a family of nomads who live solely off the land and what they can grow, forage, or preserve.

Everything around them was used to the fullest potential. Little fires in their tents served both as a heating source and as a way of cooking breads and meat. Chickens lay eggs that will later become dinner, cheese from the very few cattle they owned is stored on straw woven racks, and fruits and berries are dried out in the dessert sun to be preserved for the long treks ahead.

Here's a dish they shared with me, with a touch of desert magic.

SLOW-ROASTED LAMB SHOULDER

Peel the garlic cloves and crush them using a mortar and pestle until smooth. Add the anchovies and continue to crush to a smooth paste. Add the sabaht baharat and olive oil and stir to combine well.

Lightly score the lamb shoulder and smear the marinade all over the lamb. Place in a snug-fitting dish and cover with plastic wrap. Transfer to the fridge and leave to marinate for a day or two to let the flavors of the paste really develop.

Preheat the oven to 195°F (90°C).

Remove the marinated lamb from the fridge and place in a roasting pan. Cover tightly with parchment paper, then foil. Cook for 12 hours or until the meat falls from the bone.

NOMADS' JEWELED YOGURT

Soak the berries and currants in hot tap water for a couple of hours, then drain and set aside.

Place the yogurt in a serving bowl and garnish with all of the ingredients.

NIGELLA SEED BREAD

Put the flour, yeast, sugar, olive oil, and salt into the bowl of an electric stand mixer and combine. Attach the hook attachment, set to medium speed, gradually add 1¼ cups (300 ml) of lukewarm water, and mix for 5 minutes or until

Slow-roasted lamb shoulder

2 garlic bulbs

4 anchovy fillets

2 tablespoons sabaht baharat*
 (Lebanese 7 spice)

splash of extra virgin olive oil

1 lamb shoulder, bone in
 (about 2 lb 7 oz/1.1 kg)

Nomads' jeweled yogurt

scant 1 cup (2¾ oz/80 g) goji berries

½ cup (1¾ oz/50 g) dried golden
 berries (Incan berries)

scant ½ cup (1½ oz/40 g) barberries

½ cup (2¼ oz/60 g) dried currants

1¼ cups (10½ oz/300 g) Greek yogurt

scant ½ cup (1¾ oz/50 g) pumpkin
 seeds, toasted

⅓ cup (1¾ oz/50 g) sunflower seeds,
 toasted

¼ cup (1¾ oz/50 g) pomegranate
 seeds

2 dried apricots, finely diced

2 medjool dates, finely diced

¼ cup (1½ oz/40 g) candied orange
 and lemon peel (see note)

Nigella seed bread

3½ cups (1 lb/450 g) all-purpose
 flour, plus extra for dusting

1 envelope (¼ oz/7 g) instant yeast

1 teaspoon sugar

¼ cup (60 ml) olive oil, plus extra

1 teaspoon salt flakes, plus extra

⅓ cup (1¾ oz/50 g) nigella seeds

⅓ cup (just under 1 oz/25 g)
 coriander seeds

⅓ cup (just under 1 oz/25 g) cumin
 seeds

the dough is smooth. Alternatively you can make this dough by hand on your work surface. Put the flour on your surface, make a well in the center, add the yeast, sugar, olive oil, and salt and knead by hand. This should take 6–10 minutes to become smooth.

Place the dough in a bowl, cover with a dish towel, and leave to rest for 30 minutes to double in size.

Line a baking tray with parchment paper and preheat the oven to 375°F (190°C).

Remove the dough from the bowl and place on a floured work surface. Knock back the dough and separate into 8 even-sized portions. Knead each portion into a ball and make indents in the dough using your thumb. Transfer onto the prepared tray and drizzle with olive oil. Combine the seeds in a bowl, scatter them over the dough, and season with some more sea salt. Rest again for about 15 minutes to double in size.

Bake the bread in the oven for 10–12 minutes, until golden. Keep warm.

TO SERVE

Serve the slow-roasted lamb shoulder with the nomads' jeweled yogurt and the warm nigella seed bread.

Note This dish does require a bit of effort, and needs to be started 2 days in advance, but trust me, it's worth it.

Candied orange and lemon peel are available from specialty food stores and online.

Slow-roasted lamb shoulder
with nomads' jeweled yogurt
and nigella seed bread

ROASTED PORK BELLY WITH FENUGREEK SALAD AND ROAST GARLIC VINAIGRETTE

Salt and pork belly is a real match made in heaven. Now pork isn't something you're going to find in Iran, but as I walked through the pomegranate fields and saw wild fenugreek growing all around me, I couldn't help but think that these sweet, sour, and fresh notes would work amazingly well together and really cut the fattiness of a pork dish. So here it is.

Preheat the oven to 225°F (110°C).

Using a mortar and pestle, crush the garlic into a fine paste with the aid of some salt. Add the anchovies and continue to crush until smooth. Add the sabaht baharat and olive oil and stir through well.

Rub the bottom of the pork belly generously with the garlic mixture. Place the pork on a wire rack in a baking dish, add 1¼ cups (300 ml) of water to the dish to provide some moisture, then place in the oven and cook for 8 hours.

Meanwhile, to make the roast garlic vinaigrette, put the garlic on a baking tray and place in the oven with the pork. Roast for 30 minutes, or until soft and fragrant. Remove the garlic from the oven and squeeze out the soft roasted cloves into a small mixing bowl. Combine with the molasses, lemon juice, and a pinch of salt, and emulsify with the olive oil. Reserve until required.

Increase the oven temperature to 410°F (210°C) and cook the pork belly for a final 10–15 minutes or until the skin is crisp and crackling.

Meanwhile, to make the fenugreek salad, combine the ingredients in a bowl. Dress with the roast garlic vinaigrette.

To serve, carve the pork into individual portions. Place on four plates with the fenugreek salad and serve.

8 garlic cloves
pinch of salt flakes
6 anchovy fillets, rinsed
2 tablespoons sabaht baharat*
    (Lebanese 7 spice)
3 tablespoons extra virgin olive oil
1 lb 12 oz (800 g) piece of pork belly

Roast garlic vinaigrette

2 garlic bulbs
2 tablespoons pomegranate
    molasses*
squeeze of lemon juice
generous ¾ cup (200 ml) olive oil

Fenugreek salad

large handful fenugreek (or purslane,
    mache, or tatsoi)
5 French shallots, thinly shaved
3 radishes, thinly shaved
⅓ cup (2¼ oz/60 g) pomegranate
    seeds (optional)
generous ½ cup (2¾ oz/80 g) pine
    nuts, toasted
⅔ cup (2¼ oz/60 g) dried goji berries,
    soaked in hot water for 10 minutes
⅔ cup (2¼ oz/60 g) dried golden
    berries (Incan berries), soaked in
    hot water for 10 minutes

PISTACHIO AND BARBERRY NOUGAT DOUGHNUTS WITH ORANGE BLOSSOM SYRUP

This dish pays homage to the syrupy sweet desserts I found in Iran. Mega tasty with a little gooey surprise in the middle.

Using an electric stand mixer with the whisk attachment, whip the egg whites at a moderate speed until they begin to foam and hold stiff peaks. Continue to whisk at low speed while you make the syrup.

Combine the sugar, glucose, and ¼ cup (60 ml) of water in a saucepan over medium–high heat. Continue to cook until the mixture reaches soft ball stage—to test if the syrup is ready, drop a small amount into a shallow bowl of cold water to cool it down. It should form a soft ball. If you have a kitchen thermometer, the syrup will be ready when the temperature reaches about 240°F (115°–118°C).

Line a baking tray with parchment paper. Slowly beat the sugar syrup into the egg mixture and continue beating on low for around 20 minutes or until cool. Add the barberries and pistachios and mix until just combined. Pour the nougat onto the prepared tray and allow to set for 10 minutes.

In a small bowl, mix the cornstarch and confectioner's sugar and spread over a tray. Roll the nougat into about thirty ⅝ inch (1.5 cm) balls and place on the tray. Roll in the cornstarch and sugar mixture to coat. Cover and set aside.

To make the batter, mix the yeast and 1 cup (250 ml) of water in a large bowl. Fold in the flour, sugar, and salt, then cover with a dish towel and leave to proof in a warm place for 30 minutes or until doubled in size.

To make the orange blossom syrup, put the honey in a small saucepan and bring to a boil over high heat. As soon as it begins to boil, remove from the heat and add the orange blossom water. Set aside.

Heat the canola oil in a deep heavy-based frying pan or deep-fryer until shimmering. If you have a kitchen thermometer, the oil will be ready when the temperature reaches 340°F (170°C). Scoop out some dough, about half the size of your palm, and press a ball of nougat into the center. Turn your hand, and squeeze your fist over the surface of the hot oil. The batter should come out between your thumb and index finger in the shape of a ball. Pinch or use a knife to cut the dough encasing the nougat, allowing the doughnut to gently drop into the hot oil. Repeat to make the remaining doughnuts.

Cook in batches (you don't want to overcrowd the pan) for about 5–6 minutes until golden brown. Drain on paper towel.

Drizzle the warm orange blossom syrup over the hot doughnuts and serve.

Pistachio and barberry nougat

2 egg whites
2½ cups (1 lb 2 oz/500 g) sugar
1 cup (250 ml) liquid glucose*
⅓ cup (1¼ oz/35 g) barberries
   (or dried cranberries)
generous ½ cup (2½ oz/70 g)
   pistachios
2½ tablespoons cornstarch
2½ tablespoons confectioner's sugar

Doughnut batter

2 envelopes (½ oz/ 14 g) active dry
   yeast
2⅓ cups (10½ oz/300 g) all-purpose
   flour
2 teaspoons sugar
pinch of salt flakes
canola oil, for deep-frying

Orange blossom syrup

scant 1 cup (10½ oz/300 g) honey
scant ½ cup (100 ml) orange
   blossom water*

SAFFRON-ROASTED PEACHES WITH SAFFRON COTTON CANDY

I have always thought of saffron as one of the most feminine, gentle, and prestigious spices in the Middle Eastern kitchen. I remember softly walking through the saffron fields in Yazd, being so careful not to step on any of the little saffron flower bulbs, watching old men and women crouched over, with hands that were as worn and cracked as the dry earth of the Iranian desert, seeing the love and dedication they put into picking every strand of saffron by hand. The experience will stay with me forever and makes me appreciate this beautiful product even more.

Preheat the oven to 350°F (180°C).

Place the peaches in a baking dish and season with the saffron, vanilla, cinnamon, and bay leaves. Sprinkle with the sugar and pour in the saffron water. Roast in the oven for 20–25 minutes, or until the peaches feel soft and cooked through when pierced with a sharp knife.

Place the peaches on four serving plates. Drizzle with the pan juices, add some saffron cotton candy, and serve.

Notes You can cut the peaches in half, if you like, or use any other stone fruit.
Saffron cotton candy is available from specialist Middle Eastern grocery stores.

4 peaches
pinch of saffron threads
1 vanilla bean, split and scraped
1 cinnamon stick
2 bay leaves, torn
¾ cup (5½ oz/150 g) sugar
generous ¾ cup (200 ml) saffron water*
5½ oz (150 g) saffron cotton candy (pashmak) (see note)

TURKEY

Istanbul, Turkey

Turkey and I have a lot of history, admittedly none of which is actually firsthand. I grew up with stories on my father's knee about the Great Siege of Malta in 1565, when the Ottoman Empire tried to take my ancestral home only to be defeated by the Knights Hospitaller, the legendary warriors of Malta.

These dramatic tales of how Spanish foot soldiers and the local Maltese fought off the Sultan and his Ottoman subjects filled my little heart with a phenomenal sense of national pride: that I was descended from people from a tiny island in the Mediterranean, who could stand up to the biggest empire in the world at the time, and win.

More recently, in 1915, but under much the same heroic and heartbreaking circumstances, World War I Australian and New Zealand (ANZAC) troops were ill-fatedly deployed at the Gallipoli Peninsula. What they found waiting for them was a heavily armed and strategically positioned Turkish force, dug in and ready to defend at all costs. During that eight-month ordeal a staggering 44,000 Allies and 85,000 Turkish soldiers died, but the legacy it forged was a deep-seated respect, admiration, and generational bond. The passion, character, and camaraderie of both ANZAC and Turkish troops cemented the connection we Australians still hold with Turkey and her people today.

So what excites me the most about Turkey is probably not what excites most people when they go there, although there is an undeniable aura to the place, especially when you walk through the streets of Istanbul at sunset as the sun gently kisses the tops of the ancient and spectacular palaces dotted along the mighty Bosphorus. I remember sitting in Mandabatmaz, my absolute favorite coffee shop, watching the world drift by and seeing beaming rays of light through the city streets gradually fading into darkness, and I was captivated by all the romance, history, and greatness that Turkey once was under the Ottomans, and still is today.

Since then I have developed a deep love affair with Istanbul. She has stolen a little piece of my heart and I can't wait to return with Maha so we can both experience all the hidden secrets she still has in store.

There is an undeniable aura to the place, especially when you walk through the streets of Istanbul at sunset.

Some say that Turkey's true beauty lies in its Aegean coastline or vast Anatolian plains. Others are captivated by the otherworldly natural beauty of Cappadocia and the fairytale chimney stacks of Goreme. For others, it's when you venture into the brooding Black Sea region of the north and experience a countryside not stereotypically Turkish: rolling green hills, waterfalls, and a cuisine influenced enormously by its Georgian immigrants. But for me, the most exciting thing about Turkey isn't its fascinating history or exotic places, it is the bounty of riches it possesses in its produce. At every turn in this great land you see all the ingredients needed to become a leader in global gastronomy.

I was blown away by the quality and diversity of Turkish produce—spices, flours, oils, meats, fruits, vegetables, artisan specialty products, and techniques for preparing them that have been perfected over hundreds, if not thousands, of years—forming the backbone not only of Turkish cuisine but of Turkish culture. There is so much untapped wealth here it is hard to know where to begin, but the diverse landscape and cuisine of Turkey means that the scope of what can be grown and how it can be cooked, is enormous. Until now, the only thing holding Turkey back has been Turkey.

Much like the surrounding countries in the Middle East, Turkish food has had restricted growth. Whether it be political, religious, geographical, cultural, or historical, much of this region's food has not developed steadily over the centuries. This isn't always a bad thing—it shows purity in the cuisine and a love for something that has been perfected over thousands of years—but if you look at past and current food innovators, and their deep respect for food history, there is a potential for Turkey to develop her national cuisine to a new level and become an international force.

Here you have a rich and diverse food culture, producers and chefs who are forward thinking and adventurous, and a society that is hungry for change as well as being passionate about its heritage. All Turkey needs to do is rally her troops, fly under a united flag, and cook without fear or hesitation, and the world will be hers to conquer once more. ✖

Here you have a rich and diverse food culture, producers and chefs who are forward thinking and adventurous.

CURED SALMON WITH BEET MAYONNAISE, PUMPKIN PURÉE, AND FENNEL VINAIGRETTE

Seafood is big on the menu all down the Aegean coast of Turkey, and when it is this high quality it is pretty obvious why. Curing fish is a technique that dates back millennia on both sides of the Aegean in Greece and Turkey, and it is this tradition, along with the local fresh produce, that inspired me to make this dish.

Preheat the oven to 350°F (180°C).

Roughly chop the carrots. Put the carrots, salt, sugar, and cardamom in a food processor and mix until coarsely puréed. Place half of the mixture in the base of a large dish and lay the salmon on top. Cover well with the remaining mixture. Cover with plastic wrap and refrigerate for 3–4 hours. Wash off the cure as well as any bloodline and cut into ½ inch (1 cm) thick slices.

Meanwhile, cover a baking tray with the rock salt. Place the beets on top and cook for 45–60 minutes until tender. Remove from the oven and set aside to cool. When cool enough to handle, peel off the skin, place in a bowl, and purée using a hand-held immersion blender. Set aside.

Place the egg and egg yolks in a food processor with the mustard and lemon juice. Process until smooth. With the machine still running, slowly trickle in the blended oil until it is emulsified.

Mix equal parts of beet purée and mayonnaise. Reserve any that is leftover for another use. Transfer the beet mayonnaise into a bowl and refrigerate until required.

To make the pumpkin purée, grate the pumpkin using the largest holes of a cheese grater. Heat the butter in a saucepan over medium–low heat, then add the pumpkin. Cover with a lid and cook for 10 minutes, stirring occasionally. When the pumpkin is tender, add the cream, stir, then transfer to a food processor and blend until smooth. Set aside.

To make the fennel vinaigrette, place the vinegar and sugar in a saucepan and bring to a boil. Set aside to cool then add the micro fennel.

To serve, place a slice of salmon on each serving plate. Dress with the fennel vinaigrette, extra virgin olive oil, and some salt. Add dollops of the beet mayonnaise and pumpkin purée. Garnish with some fennel fronds. Serve immediately.

Note If you can't get micro fennel, slice small fennel bulbs into thin lengths.

Cured salmon

5 carrots, peeled
½ cup (4½ oz/125 g) table salt
generous 1 cup (7¾ oz/220 g) sugar
½ cup (2½ oz/70 g) cardamom pods, cracked open and toasted
1 side sashimi-grade salmon (about 1 lb 12 oz/800 g), pin boned, skin removed

Beet mayonnaise

1 lb 2 oz (500 g) kosher salt (about 1½ cups, depending on brand)
1 lb 2 oz (500 g) beets
1 egg
5 egg yolks
2½ tablespoons dijon mustard
3 tablespoons lemon juice
2½ cups (600 ml) blended oil (50:50 vegetable oil and olive oil)

Pumpkin purée

1 lb 2 oz (500 g) kabocha squash (or other winter squash)
5½ tablespoons (2¾ oz/80 g) butter
⅔ cup (150 ml) whipping cream

Fennel vinaigrette

1¼ cups (300 ml) chardonnay vinegar
2 cups (10½ oz/300 g) light brown sugar
8 micro fennel (or 2 small fennel bulbs), thinly sliced, plus extra fronds to serve (see note)

splash of extra virgin olive oil
pinch of salt flakes

SCALLOP-FILLED ZUCCHINI FLOWERS WITH SMOKED EEL DRESSING AND ORANGE AND CORIANDER CRUMB

I found flowers growing wild throughout Turkey, and in Bodrum it inspired me to use vegetable flowers in my cooking. This dish is one of the results.

Put the rice in a small saucepan with enough water to cover by ½ inch (1 cm). Bring to a boil, cover with a lid, and cook for 12–15 minutes until the water is absorbed and the rice is plump and tender.

Heat the olive oil in a frying pan over medium–high heat. Add the onion and sauté for a few minutes until translucent. Add the pine nuts, cooked rice, and lemon zest. Stir to mix and then remove from the heat. Add the scallops, cheeses, and mint and stir through.

Fill the zucchini flowers with the scallop filling and gently fold or twist the opening shut. Place on a tray, cover with plastic wrap, and refrigerate.

To make the crumb, combine the orange zest, breadcrumbs, and coriander seeds in a shallow bowl. Lightly coat the filled zucchini flowers in the flour, dip in the beaten egg, then roll in the breadcrumbs to evenly cover. Transfer to a plate, cover with plastic wrap, and refrigerate to rest.

Meanwhile, to make the smoked eel dressing, flake the eel meat into a mixing bowl, add the remaining ingredients, and check the seasoning. Set aside.

Pour some sunflower oil into a deep frying pan, about 1½ inches (4 cm) deep, then heat over medium–high heat until it shimmers. If you have a kitchen thermometer, the oil will be ready when the temperature reaches 350°F (180°C). Alternatively, use a deep-fryer. Remove the zucchini flowers from the fridge and carefully add to the pan, a few at a time, then cook for 2–3 minutes until all the sides are golden brown, turning as necessary. Drain on paper towels.

Divide the zucchini flowers between four serving plates. Drizzle with the smoked eel dressing and serve immediately.

Note Pumpkin flowers actually work best for this dish but aren't always easy to find, so we've used the more available zucchini flowers instead, as an easy replacement.

Scallop-filled zucchini flowers

½ cup (3¾ oz/110 g) baldo rice (or arborio rice)
2½ tablespoons olive oil
1 yellow onion, finely diced
2½ tablespoons pine nuts, toasted
zest of 1 lemon
12 scallops, roe removed, quartered
2¾ oz (80 g) haloumi cheese, finely grated
1¼ cups (4¼ oz/120 g) finely grated kefalograviera (or parmesan) cheese
small handful mint, leaves picked and torn
12 zucchini flowers, buds removed (or use pumpkin flowers, see note)
sunflower oil, for deep-frying

Orange and coriander crumb

zest of 1 orange
2¾ cups (10½ oz/300 g) dry breadcrumbs
3 tablespoons coriander seeds, crushed
all-purpose flour, for dusting
2 eggs, beaten

Smoked eel dressing

½ smoked eel (about 7 oz/200 g), meat picked from bone and skin
2 French shallots, finely diced
2½ tablespoons sherry vinegar
1 cup (250 ml) olive oil
1 tablespoon Aleppo pepper*
large handful Italian parsley leaves, roughly torn

CEMEN CURED BLUE EYE PASTIRMA WITH TARAMASALATA

A popular process for preserving meat, called pastirma in Turkey, involves covering meat in a spice paste (cemen) and leaving it to cure. It's a technique that many nationalities lay claim to around the Mediterranean and Baltic seas, but, to be honest, I don't care where it originated as long as it tastes great, and the pastirma I had in Turkey was AMAZING!

Curing meat can be a long and risky process if you get it wrong. This is a really simple recipe that has all the big flavors of a traditional meat pastirma, but brings some new life to it with the introduction of fish. It is a lot easier to make as well.

Combine all the dry curing ingredients with the orange zest in a large bowl.

Place half the mixture on the base of a large rectangular tray. Place the fish on top and cover with the remaining mixture, pressing it down onto the blue eye. Cover with plastic wrap then place in the fridge and allow to cure for 6 hours.

Quickly rinse the fish under cold running water to remove any excess curing mixture, leaving a thin layer of spice still attached. Slice the blue eye into ¼ inch (5 mm) slices and keep refrigerated until required.

Put the bread in a bowl, cover with 1¼ cups (300 ml) of water, and leave to soak for 10 minutes. Remove the bread and squeeze out the water.

Blend the onion in a food processor. Add the soaked bread and process until smooth. Add the cod roe and lemon juice, and process until smooth. While the machine is running, slowly drizzle in the olive oil, a little at a time. Season the taramasalata with salt to taste. (See note.)

Place slices of fish in the middle of a large platter. Add dollops of taramasalata, chives, radish, and the micro cress, if using, and serve.

Note Instead of taramasalata, you could also serve the cemen cured blue eye with Kewpie mayonnaise.

Cured blue eye pastirma

½ cup (2¾ oz/80 g) ground fenugreek
¾ cup (2¾ oz/80 g) smoked paprika
3 tablespoons ground coriander
3 tablespoons ground cumin
5½ oz (150 g) salt flakes (about 1¼ cups, depending on brand)
¾ cup (5½ oz/150 g) sugar
zest of 1 orange
1 side blue-eye trevalla (Antarctic butterfish), skin, bone, and bloodline removed

Taramasalata

4 slices white bread, crusts removed
½ onion, roughly chopped
3½ oz (100 g) white cod roe paste
2½ tablespoons lemon juice
2 cups (500 ml) olive oil
pinch of salt flakes

handful chives, cut into ¾ inch (2 cm) lengths
1 radish, very thinly sliced
micro cress (optional)

Preparation time: 30 minutes • Cooking time: 30 minutes • Serves: 4

VILLAGE-STYLE FETA BOREK WITH SMOKED EGGPLANT MAYONNAISE

When I was in Turkey I picked up a great trick for making borek, using sparkling mineral water with the oil to brush over the pastries. This really is the difference between the amazing boreks I had in Turkey and the ones I'd been cooking at home. Another tip is to make sure you add a little salt to the egg mix—it adds a bit of crunch to the finished product.

Fry the diced sucuk in a large frying pan, over medium heat, until crispy and golden. Remove the sucuk from the heat and stir in the feta and parsley.

Combine the olive oil and salt in small bowl with the mineral water and stir.

Carefully cut each sheet of pastry into 8 triangle shapes. Place a tablespoon of the sucuk mixture in the middle of each pastry triangle, about ¾ inch (2 cm) from the edge. Brush the pastry with the olive oil and water mixture and roll the pastry tightly around the filling, folding in the sides to create a cylinder shape, to make 16 boreks.

To make the smoked eggplant mayonnaise, place the whole eggplants over a gas flame, on the grill, or under the broiler, and cook until the skin is charred and the flesh is soft. Set aside to cool, then remove the skin and cut the flesh into rough chunks.

Place the egg and egg yolks in a food processor with the mustard and lemon juice. Process until smooth. With the machine still running, slowly trickle in the blended oil until it is all emulsified. Add the eggplant, Aleppo pepper, lemon zest, tahini, and salt to taste, and continue to process until smooth.

Pour some into a deep frying pan to a depth of about 1½ inches (4 cm), then heat over medium–high heat until it shimmers. If you have a kitchen thermometer, the oil will be ready when the temperature reaches 350°F (180°C). Alternatively, use a deep-fryer. Carefully add the boreks to the pan and cook for 2–3 minutes until golden brown. Transfer onto paper towels to drain.

Serve the village-style feta borek hot with the smoked eggplant mayonnaise.

Feta borek

9 oz (250 g) sucuk sausages*, diced small

1 cup (5½ oz/150 g) crumbled feta cheese

handful Italian parsley, leaves picked and torn

1 cup (250 ml) olive oil

2½ tablespoons salt flakes

½ cup (120 ml) sparkling mineral water

2 sheets yufka pastry (or filo pastry)

canola oil, for deep-frying

Smoked eggplant mayonnaise

2 eggplants

1 egg

5 egg yolks

2½ tablespoons dijon mustard

3 tablespoons lemon juice

4 cups (1 liter) blended oil (50:50 vegetable oil and olive oil)

heaped 1 tablespoon Aleppo pepper*

zest of 1 lemon

2½ tablespoons tahini*

pinch of salt flakes

STUFFED MUSSELS WITH PRESERVED LEMON DRESSING

Everywhere you go in Istanbul there is a mussel dish on the menu. Two of the best I experienced had to have been fried mussels on a stick, and stuffed mussels with rice. This dish brings together elements of both in a really tasty combination.

First, cook the mussels. Heat the olive oil and butter in a saucepan over medium–high heat, add the French shallots, garlic, thyme, and bay leaf, and sauté for a few minutes until translucent. Add the mussels and white wine and cook for 30–60 seconds or until the mussels start to open. Strain into a colander to cool over a bowl and set aside.

To make the rice filling, put the rice in a saucepan with enough water to cover by ½ inch (1 cm). Bring to a boil, cover with a lid, and cook for 12–15 minutes until the water has been absorbed and the rice is plump and tender.

Melt the butter in a frying pan over medium heat. Add the pine nuts and stir until golden brown. Add the currants and sabaht baharat and stir. Tear the parsley leaves and add these to the pan with the cooked rice, season with salt, then turn out onto a tray and leave to cool.

Remove the mussels from their shells, making sure the beards have been removed, and fill with the rice filling. Refrigerate for at least 30 minutes.

Put the cornstarch and 1¼ cups (5½ oz/150 g) of the flour into a mixing bowl and combine. Using a whisk, slowly add the mineral water to make a smooth pouring consistency batter, but make sure the batter is thick enough to coat the mussels.

To make the preserved lemon dressing, combine the ingredients in a small bowl and set aside.

Pour some sunflower oil into a deep frying pan, about 1½ inches (4 cm) deep, then heat over medium–high heat until it shimmers. If you have a kitchen thermometer, the oil will be ready when the temperature reaches 350°F (180°C). Alternatively, use a deep-fryer.

Coat the stuffed mussels with the remaining ½ cup (2½ oz/75 g) of flour, dip in the tempura batter, then shake off the excess. Carefully place the battered mussels into the pan, a few at a time, and cook for 1–2 minutes, then remove and place on paper towels to soak up the oil. Repeat with the remaining mussels.

Place the cooked mussels on a plate and dress with the preserved lemon dressing. Serve immediately.

Mussels

2½ tablespoons olive oil
2 tablespoons (1 oz/30 g) butter
2 French shallots, thinly sliced
1 garlic clove, thinly sliced
5 thyme sprigs
1 bay leaf, torn
2 lb 4 oz (1 kg) mussels, cleaned
1 cup (250 ml) dry white wine

Rice filling

½ cup (3¾ oz/110 g) baldo rice
   (or arborio rice)
2 tablespoons (1 oz/30 g) butter
2½ tablespoons pine nuts
2½ tablespoons dried currants
heaped 1 tablespoon sabaht baharat*
   (Lebanese 7 spice)
small handful Italian parsley, leaves
   picked
pinch of salt

Tempura batter

2 cups (9 oz/250 g) cornstarch
1¾ cups (8 oz/225 g) all-purpose flour
2 cups (500 ml) sparkling mineral
   water
sunflower oil, for deep-frying

Preserved lemon dressing

1 tablespoon finely diced French
   shallot
2½ tablespoons diced preserved
   lemon peel
1 teaspoon Aleppo pepper*
⅓ cup (80 ml) olive oil
2½ tablespoons sherry vinegar

MOREL, SWISS CHARD, AND DUCK GOZLEME WITH MOREL BUTTER

I was really surprised to find so much game, mushrooms, and fresh produce in the hills surrounding Fethiye and around the Bodrum Peninsula. It really wasn't the Turkey I was expecting to find and reminded me a lot more of Europe than Anatolia. This gozleme dish unites many of these ingredients.

To make the gozleme dough, put the flour, salt, sugar, olive oil, and 1⅓ cups (325 ml) of water into the bowl of an electric stand mixer. Attach the dough hook and mix at low speed for 7 minutes or until combined. Cover the bowl with a dish towel and place in a warm spot for 30 minutes to double in size.

To make the morel butter, combine all the ingredients in a food processor and process until smooth. Set aside.

To make the morel, Swiss chard, and duck filling, heat the butter in a frying pan over medium heat. Add the onion and sauté for a few minutes until translucent. Add the morels, bay leaf, and rosemary and stir. As the morels become crispier, add the ground cumin and stir to mix. Tip out onto a tray to cool.

Combine the Swiss chard, kale, duck, feta, Aleppo pepper, and 1 tablespoon of the morel butter with the sautéed ingredients in a large bowl. Mix well, then set aside.

Sprinkle some flour on your work surface and divide the gozleme dough into 10 portions. Roll out the dough portions into 6 inch (15 cm) flat rounds, 1/16 inch (2 mm) thick. Place a good even layer of the duck mixture on one half, leaving a ½ inch (1 cm) border from the edge of the pastry. Fold over and seal the rim.

Place 2 tablespoons of the remaining morel butter onto a flat griddle over medium–high heat (see note). Place a few gozleme on top to cook, brushing the tops with more morel butter. When the pastry is golden, after 2–3 minutes, turn over and cook for a further 2–3 minutes. Repeat with the remaining gozleme.

Serve immediately.

Note You can also use a frying pan, barbecue, or pizza stone to cook the gozleme.

Gozleme dough

4 cups (1 lb 2 oz/500 g) all-purpose flour, plus extra for dusting
pinch of salt flakes
pinch of sugar
splash of olive oil

Morel butter

1 cup (1¾ oz/50 g) dried morels, soaked for at least 15 minutes
11 tablespoons (5½ oz/150 g) butter, at room temperature
pinch of salt flakes
2 tablespoons olive oil

Morel, Swiss chard, and duck filling

2 tablespoons (1 oz/30 g) butter
1 large yellow onion, finely chopped
2 cups (3½ oz/100 g) dried morels, soaked for at least 15 minutes, roughly chopped
1 bay leaf, torn
1 rosemary sprig
1 teaspoon ground cumin
3 Swiss chard leaves, stem removed, finely chopped
3 lacinato kale leaves, finely chopped
9 oz (250 g) ground duck
1 cup (5½ oz/150 g) crumbled feta cheese
heaped 1 tablespoon Aleppo pepper*

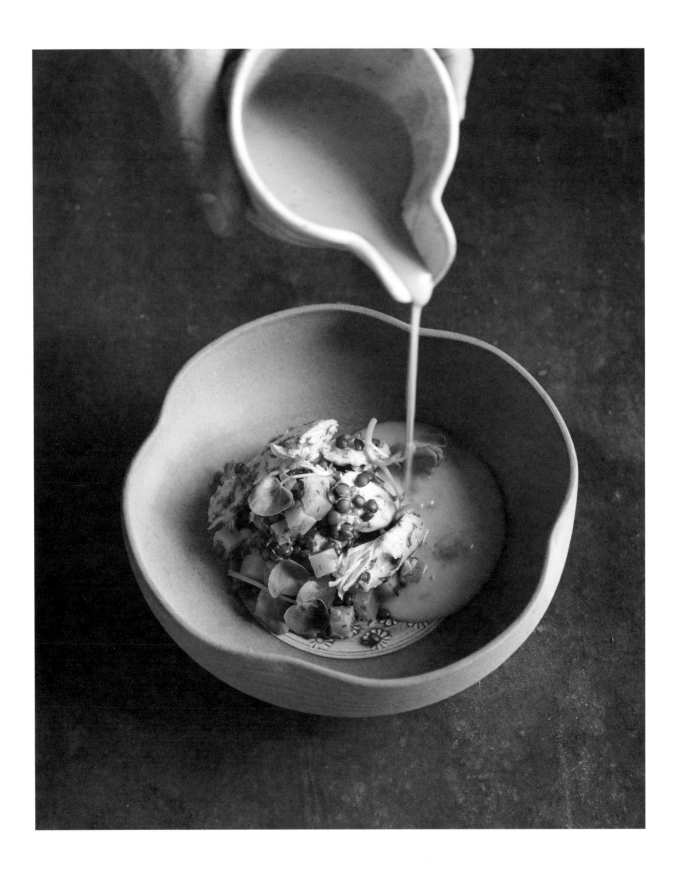

SMOKED TROUT TRAHANA

This would have to be where food companies stole the idea for instant soup! This is a great dish with tons of flavor that I haven't changed very much from the original I tried in Turkey. The smoked rainbow trout is the only substantial difference, helping to lift what was already a superb dish.

Bring a small saucepan of water to a boil, add the lentils, and cook for 15 minutes or until just tender. Drain and set aside.

Bring 6 cups (1.5 liters) of water to a boil in a saucepan over medium–high heat. Pour ½ cup (120 ml) of the water from the pan into a bowl and add the trahana, then pour it back into the pan. Stir for 3–4 minutes, add the butter, and season to taste. Set aside.

Combine all the vegetables, the lentils, Aleppo pepper, and smoked trout in a mixing bowl. Arrange a small amount in the middle of each serving bowl, scatter the watercress on top, pour in the soup, and serve.

Notes Trahana is a soup base made from cracked grains and fermented yogurt, which is dried and then ground into a powder. It is available from specialist Middle Eastern grocery stores.

You can substitute smoked salmon for the trout.

¼ cup (2 oz/55 g) French (Puy) lentils
1 cup (5½ oz/150 g) trahana (see note)
7 tablespoons (3½ oz/100 g) butter
1 small celery stalk, finely diced
1 carrot, peeled and finely diced
1 small turnip, peeled and finely diced
1 teaspoon Aleppo pepper*
5½ oz (150 g) smoked rainbow trout, skin removed, flesh flaked from the bone (see note)
handful watercress, leaves picked

LAMB SHANK KEBAB

Traditionally, this dish is cooked in a tandoori-style oven that is built into the floor of central Anatolian kitchens. The clay for the pot it is cooked in is sourced from a local river that has a high mineral content and in turn this leaches a salty, earthy flavor into the finished dish. But never fear, this recipe, simply cooked in a heavy-based Dutch oven, produces a beautiful result. It may not have the romance of the original, but it saves you digging up your kitchen floor to build the oven. Enjoy!

Soak the dried beans in separate bowls of water overnight. Drain and set aside.

Combine the garlic, rosemary, 3 tablespoons of the Aleppo pepper, and the salt using a mortar and pestle. Rub the mixture onto the lamb shanks to evenly coat. Place the shanks in a non-metallic bowl, cover with plastic wrap, and refrigerate for at least 4 hours to marinate.

Preheat the oven to 315°F (160°C).

Seal the lamb shanks in a Dutch oven over medium–high heat, on all sides until golden brown. Add the spices and 2 remaining tablespoons of Aleppo pepper to the dish and cook for 1 minute. Add the pastes and stir, then add the carrots, onions, soaked beans, and tomatoes. Add the stock to just cover the meat, cover the dish with a lid, and cook for 3 hours, or until the meat falls from the bones.

Remove the dish from the oven, stir in the kale, top with the walnuts and lemon zest, and serve.

Note Use lamb leg or shoulder if you can't get shanks.

1 cup (7 oz/200 g) dried navy beans

1 cup (7 oz/200 g) dried borlotti beans

2 garlic bulbs, cloves peeled and crushed

2 rosemary sprigs

5 tablespoons Aleppo pepper*

pinch of salt flakes

6 lamb shanks (about 10½ oz/300 g each) (see note)

3 cinnamon sticks

heaped 1 tablespoon ground cumin

heaped 1 tablespoon ground coriander

2½ tablespoons red pepper paste*

2½ tablespoons tomato paste

2 carrots, peeled and quartered

12 cocktail onions

6 vine-ripened tomatoes, quartered

8 cups (2 liters) lamb stock (or another meat stock)

8 lacinato kale leaves

¾ cup (2½ oz/70 g) walnuts, toasted and crushed

zest of 1 lemon

Istiklal Avenue, Taksim, Istanbul

PASTIRMA, SHRIMP, AND FETA PIDE

Now the debate over who invented the pizza is one I'll leave to others. All I care about is if it is good or not. I love a traditional Neapolitan-style pizza, and Turkish- and Lebanese-style spiced lamb flatbreads are foods that get my heart pumping and are probably responsible for about five pounds of my belly fat. But I have to admit that Turkish pide at its best is something not to be messed with. Light, airy, crispy pastry that holds together endless amounts of flavor. Sitting by the Bosphorus devouring a fresh pide and washing it down with a few Turkish beers—I can't really think of anything better.

Combine the dough ingredients and scant ½ cup (100 ml) of lukewarm water in an electric stand mixer. Attach the dough hook and knead for 3–5 minutes at a moderate–high speed, until the dough is smooth and starts to come away from the bowl. Cover with a dish towel and set aside to proof in a warm spot for 30 minutes or until the dough doubles in size.

Combine the shrimp, feta, kale, spices, lemon zest, and parsley in a large bowl. Cover with plastic wrap and refrigerate until required.

Place a pizza stone or baking tray in the oven and preheat to 425°F (220°C).

Sprinkle some flour on your work surface. Divide the dough into 2 portions and then use a rolling pin and roll each portion into a rectangle shape. Divide the filling evenly into 2 portions and put these in the middle of each dough portion, then fold over the edges and pinch at either end. Place the pastirma slices down the center.

Place the pides on the preheated stone or baking tray and cook for 8–10 minutes until golden.

Serve hot with lemon wedges.

Notes You can use dried yeast if fresh is not available. Generally, you require half the quantity. Here, use just under half an envelope instant yeast, or use half an envelope active dry yeast, but dissolve it in the water before adding.

Pastirma is a Middle Eastern cured meat, available from delicatessens and specialist Middle Eastern grocery stores. If pastirma isn't really your thing, you can substitute any other cured meat—Spanish jamon would work well.

Pide dough

⅛ oz (5 g) fresh yeast (see note to use dried)
1 teaspoon sugar
1 cup (5½ oz/150 g) bread flour, plus extra for dusting
1 teaspoon salt flakes

10 large raw shrimp, peeled and deveined, tails removed
1 cup (5½ oz/150 g) crumbled feta cheese
5 lacinato kale leaves, blanched and torn
1 teaspoon Aleppo pepper*
1 teaspoon fennel seeds
1 teaspoon ground coriander
zest of 1 lemon
large handful Italian parsley, leaves picked
3½ oz (100 g) pastirma, cut into 1⁄16 inch (2 mm) slices (see note)
lemon wedges, to serve

ALI NAZIK LAMB KOFTE WITH EGGPLANT YOGURT AND BLACK BREAD GARNISH

This is one of the dishes that really defines Turkish food for me. Beautiful coal-grilled lamb with smoky, silky eggplant and a spicy butter sauce. I could eat this dish every day for the rest of my life and be a very happy man. By far the best Ali Nazik dish I tasted was in Gaziantep at one of my all-time favorite restaurants, Imam Cagdas. You can't go to Turkey and not eat there. The baklava served in the street-front pastry shop is the best there is, and the food served in the restaurant upstairs is out of this world.

Combine the lamb, tail fat, Aleppo pepper, and garlic in a bowl and mix well. Divide into 4 even-sized balls and thread onto four skewers in a barrel shape, distributing evenly. Cover with plastic wrap and refrigerate.

Meanwhile, place the whole eggplants over a gas flame or barbecue and cook until the skin is well charred and the flesh is soft. Set aside to cool, then remove the skin and cut the flesh into rough chunks. Transfer to a food processor and blend until smooth (see note).

Combine the puréed eggplant with the yogurt in a bowl, and then fold in the purslane.

To make the black bread garnish, melt the butter in a frying pan over high heat. When the butter begins to foam, add the red pepper paste and stir well. Roughly break up the black bread and add it to the pan. Add the almonds, Aleppo pepper, lemon juice, and parsley, and stir. Set aside.

Preheat your grill or grill pan to medium–high. Remove the lamb skewers from the fridge.

Cook the kofte for 3–4 minutes on each side until cooked through evenly. Carefully remove from the skewers and cut each one into 3 pieces.

Pool some eggplant yogurt onto each serving plate. Add the kofte and top with the bread garnish and pan juices. Serve immediately.

Notes You can keep the eggplant pieces chunky instead of puréed if you prefer. Purslane can be found in some farmer's markets but also grows wild across much of North America.

Lamb kofte
9 oz (250 g) ground lean lamb shoulder
1¾ oz (50 g) lamb tail fat* (or suet or lard)
heaped 1 tablespoon Aleppo pepper*
1 large garlic clove, crushed

Eggplant yogurt
3 eggplants
generous ¾ cup (7 oz/200 g) Greek yogurt
small handful purslane (see note) (or fresh fenugreek or lamb's lettuce)

Black bread garnish
2 tablespoons (1 oz/30 g) butter
1 tablespoon red pepper paste*
black bread (see page 124)
½ cup (1¾ oz/50 g) sliced almonds, toasted
1 teaspoon Aleppo pepper*
squeeze of lemon juice
small handful Italian parsley, leaves picked and torn

BLACK BREAD

Now, this bread recipe isn't traditionally Turkish. The reason I wanted to include it is because, for me, the best meat and kofte is always cooked over coal, but not all of us can have the luxury of having a coal grill set-up. So this bread is the next best thing. When you tear the baked bread and fry it in butter, lemon, and a little spice it becomes dark and crunchy and looks like chunks of coal. And of course, smoky eggplant and grilled meat isn't complete without some bread to mop it up with.

Combine the milk, yeast and ⅓ cup (75 ml) of lukewarm water in the bowl of an electric stand mixer. Attach the dough hook and mix at a moderate speed until the yeast has dissolved. Add the flours, salt, and food coloring and knead for 3–6 minutes until smooth. Cover with a dish towel and leave to rest in a warm place for 45–60 minutes until doubled in size.

Sprinkle some flour on your work surface. Separate the dough into 2 portions and use a rolling pin to roll them into your desired loaf shapes. Allow to proof in a warm spot again for 30 minutes.

Preheat the oven to 400°F (200°C).

Place the bread on two trays and bake for 15–20 minutes until cooked. You can tell if the bread is ready by tapping the base. If it sounds hollow, the bread is cooked.

Notes This bread freezes really well and can be used to make hamburger buns and other bread shapes—a real eye catcher at those special events.

Black food coloring can be found at specialty food stores and online. The amount you need will vary by brand, so add it slowly, mix, and see if you need more. You can also make the bread without it—it will still be delicious.

scant ½ cup (100 ml) milk, at room temperature
1 teaspoon fresh yeast
¾ cup (3½ oz/100 g) all-purpose flour, plus extra for dusting
1 cup (5½ oz/150 g) bread flour
pinch of salt flakes
black food coloring (optional) (see note)

VINE LEAF-WRAPPED QUAIL, SUCUK, AND CANDIED WALNUTS AND FIGS

Traveling through the bazaars in Turkey can be an overwhelming experience—so much to see, so much to buy, and so many new flavors and textures to experience. One product I found in the bazaars was candied walnuts, and I couldn't wait to use them.

Wrapping foods in vine leaves is a popular Middle Eastern technique to hold in the natural juices in a dish. This is a great recipe to make your own—really easy and very tasty.

Put the rice in a small saucepan with enough water to cover by ½ inch (1 cm). Bring to a boil, cover with a lid, and cook for 12–15 minutes until the water is absorbed and the rice is plump and tender. Preheat the oven to 500°F (250°C).

Remove the casing from 1 lb 2 oz (500 g) of the sucuk and set aside the rest. Put the sucuk meat, rice, chopped rosemary, and parsley stems in a bowl and mix until well combined. Divide into 6 even-sized balls. Mold the quail around the balls and then wrap in vine leaves. Thread two skewers into each end of the quails and place on a baking tray.

Bake for 8–10 minutes until golden. Remove from the oven and set aside, lightly covered, to rest.

Meanwhile, dice the remaining 3 oz (100 g) of sucuk and place in a saucepan over medium–high heat. Sauté for a few minutes until crispy, then add the rosemary lengths and toss through until aromatic. Add the figs and walnuts with a generous drizzle of the syrups, bring to a boil, then remove from the heat.

Remove the skewers from the quail and cut each quail in half. Place on serving plates, spoon on some of the the walnut, fig, and sucuk garnish, top with rosemary, and serve.

Note Jarred grape vine leaves, candied figs, and candied walnuts are available at specialist Middle Eastern grocery stores. They can also be purchased online.

⅓ cup (2¼ oz/60 g) baldo rice (or arborio rice)

1 lb 5 oz (600 g) sucuk sausages*

heaped 1 tablespoon chopped rosemary leaves

handful Italian parsley, leaves picked, stems chopped

6 jumbo quails (about 6 oz/175 g each), backbone removed, wings and drumstick intact

16 vine leaves (see note)

1 rosemary sprig, broken into 6 lengths

6 candied figs, with syrup (see note)

6 candied walnuts, with syrup (see note)

Cappadocia, Turkey

Preparation time: 25 minutes • Cooking time: 35 minutes • Serves: 6

WILD GREENS WITH SUCUK BALLS AND EGGS

This is a great dish to share with the family. Just serve it with a bowl of yogurt and some crusty bread for breakfast, lunch, or dinner. You can use other leaves in this dish, besides chicory and Swiss chard. Lacinato kale or even some Asian greens would work well.

Combine all the sucuk ball ingredients in a bowl. Season generously with salt and pepper. Add a generous 1 tablespoon of water and mix thoroughly until well combined. Roll into about 60 balls and set aside.

Preheat the oven to 400°F (200°C).

Blanch the chicory and Swiss chard leaves in a saucepan of boiling salted water over medium–high heat for 5 minutes. Drain and set aside.

Meanwhile, heat 1 tablespoon of the olive oil in a large frying pan over medium–high heat. Add the sucuk balls, in batches, and sauté for a few minutes until evenly browned and caramelized, adding more oil as required. Transfer onto paper towels to absorb any excess oil. Add the onions and garlic to the pan and cook for a few minutes until golden, then add the butter and allow to foam. Add the chicory and Swiss chard stems, then add the blanched leaves. Season with the Aleppo pepper, then transfer, with the sucuk balls, to a shallow baking dish. Crack the eggs straight into the dish and bake in the oven for 3–5 minutes or until the egg whites are cooked and the yolk is still a little runny.

Serve immediately, straight from the dish, with yogurt and crusty bread.

Sucuk balls

2 lb 4 oz (1 kg) coarsely ground beef
9 oz (250 g) coarsely ground lamb tail fat* (or suet or lard)
3 garlic cloves
3 tablespoons sweet paprika
heaped 1 tablespoon ground cumin

6 chicory stems, leaves picked, stems roughly chopped
6 Swiss chard stems, leaves separated, stems roughly chopped
⅓ cup (80 ml) olive oil
2 yellow onions, thinly sliced
4 garlic cloves, crushed
2 tablespoons (1 oz/30 g) butter
heaped 1 tablespoon Aleppo pepper*
6 eggs
Greek yogurt and crusty bread, to serve

BRAISED LAMB WITH SALTBUSH AND CANTALOUPE

This is a dish that you are going to want to cook over and over. Dead simple and packed full of flavor. For me a slow-roasted lamb shoulder is one of the best meat dishes you can cook—full of flavor, moisture and so satisfying to eat and serve to your friends and family. Long and slow is the way to go with this recipe. All the work is in the preparation of the meat and then it's just a matter of putting it in the oven and letting it go to work.

If you can't get saltbush don't worry. It adds real mineral earth saltiness to the dish, but you can make do without it. The real surprise in this dish is the caramelized cantaloupe. The sweetness in the dish is a real knockout, especially with the introduction of fresh herbs, Aleppo pepper, and lemon juice.

Place the lamb in a large wide-based saucepan over high heat and cook, turning occasionally to brown, for 10 minutes. Add the garlic, exposed side down, onion, and spices and continue to cook for 5 minutes until the lamb is evenly sealed and the onion is caramelized. Add the saltbush, if using, and enough stock to cover. Bring to a boil, then reduce the heat to a simmer. Cover with a lid and braise for 3–4 hours or until the meat falls off the bone.

Remove the bone from the lamb and discard. Set the meat aside and keep warm. Increase the heat to high and continue to cook the braising liquid for about 20 minutes until reduced by half. Remove about ½ cup (120 ml) of the sauce and set aside. Return the lamb to the pan.

Meanwhile, remove the skin and seeds from the melon and cut the flesh into ¾ inch (2 cm) pieces. Place the melon in a dry frying pan over high heat and caramelize for a few minutes, tossing to cook on all sides (see note). Add the raisins, pine nuts, cilantro, mint, and lemon zest. Mix until combined and add the reserved sauce to help bind the cantaloupe and garnishes together.

Season to taste, and serve the lamb with the melon salad.

Notes Saltbush is an edible shrub in the *atriplex* genus, found in dry inland Australia and growing wild along North American coastlines. It has a pleasant salty flavor.

The pan has to be really hot to caramelize the melon, otherwise it will stew in its juices.

1 lamb shoulder (about 2 lb 7 oz/ 1.1 kg), bone in
1 garlic bulb, halved crossways
2 yellow onions, roughly chopped
heaped 1 tablespoon ground cumin
heaped 1 tablespoon ground coriander
heaped 1 tablespoon Aleppo pepper*
2 large handfuls saltbush (optional) (see note)
8–12 cups (2–3 liters) lamb stock (or another meat stock)
½ cantaloupe
½ cup (3 oz/85 g) raisins
1¾ cups (8½ oz/235 g) pine nuts, toasted
handful cilantro, leaves picked and chopped
handful mint, leaves picked and chopped
zest of 1 lemon

WAGYU BEEF MANTI WITH PEAS, PICKLED ONIONS, AND GARLIC YOGURT

It's the eternal debate—who invented pasta? Well, all I know is that the Turkish "pasta," manti, is a damn tasty version. While I was in Kayseri I had the pleasure of learning how to make the tiniest little manti I have ever seen. The ladies who taught me told me that the true test of good manti is to be able to fit 40 pieces on each spoon! Well, there is no way I could ever make them that small with my fat fingers, or as tasty as they did, but the version below is a pretty good try.

Mix the manti dough ingredients together with ½ cup (120 ml) of water in the bowl of an electric stand mixer. Using the dough hook attachment, knead at a low speed for 3–6 minutes until a smooth ball is formed. Cover with a dish towel and leave to rest for 30 minutes.

Combine all the wagyu beef filling ingredients in a bowl.

Sprinkle some flour on your work surface and on a tray. Using a rolling pin, flatten the dough to ⅟₁₆ inch (2 mm) thick. Cut the dough into ⅝ inch (1.5 cm) squares. Place a tiny amount of filling in the middle of each piece of dough, then bring up all 4 edges to make a diamond shape. Pinch the edges to seal them shut. Repeat this process until all the filling has been used. Place the dumplings on the floured tray (see note).

Combine the garlic yogurt ingredients in a bowl, cover with plastic wrap, and refrigerate until required.

Bring a saucepan of salted water to a boil over high heat. Add the manti and blanch for 2–4 minutes or until they start to float on the surface.

Melt the butter in a large frying pan over medium–high heat. Add the diced sucuk and sauté for a few minutes. Add the peas and pickled onions and stir. Add the manti, but don't discard the blanching water.

Put the red pepper paste in a bowl, add a ladleful of the manti blanching water, and stir rigorously. Add this to the frying pan and allow to bubble for 2 minutes.

Divide the dumplings between four serving bowls. Top with some garlic yogurt and mint leaves, sprinkle with some Aleppo pepper, and serve.

Notes Get the kids involved in making these, since small hands are good for this job. They're time consuming, so make a large batch and freeze the excess. These can also be frozen if you want to prep them ahead of time, just freeze on a floured tray. When frozen, you can place in freezer bags.

Manti dough
1⅔ cups (9 oz/250 g) bread flour, plus extra for dusting
1 egg
pinch of salt flakes

Wagyu beef filling
3½ oz (100 g) ground wagyu beef (or other good quality ground beef)
1 garlic clove, crushed
pinch of Aleppo pepper*

Garlic yogurt
generous ¾ cup (7 oz/200 g) Greek yogurt
1 garlic clove, crushed
pinch of salt flakes

1 tablespoon (½ oz/15 g) butter
3½ oz (100 g) sucuk sausages*, diced
⅔ cup (3½ oz/100 g) fresh peas
3½ oz (100 g) pickled cocktail onions
2½ tablespoons red pepper paste*
10 mint leaves, torn
pinch of Aleppo pepper*

Preparation time: 1 hour, plus overnight soaking • Cooking time: 15 minutes • Serves: 4

ROAST CHICKPEA HUMMUS WITH LAMB KEBAB

On the southeastern border of Turkey lies the town of Mardin—a lonely forgotten plot of land many people claim as home. There is a huge Syrian community and influence in this part of Turkey, so much so that the food and the language is different from the rest of the country. One night, after the cameras were switched off and it was time for dinner, I wandered into a little Syrian/Turkish restaurant. They brought out an array of mezze and I was blown away by this roast chickpea hummus—so nutty, so texturally different from any hummus I had ever had before. I had to cook it and share it with you.

Preheat the oven to 400°F (200°C).

Drain the soaked chickpeas and boil them in twice their volume of water until tender (up to an hour). Drain, let them cool completely, and pat dry. Toss in a splash of olive oil to coat and some salt, then arrange in one layer on a baking tray. Roast for about 30 minutes until browned.

To make the roast chickpea hummus, combine the roast chickpeas, garlic, tahini, lemon juice, a splash of olive oil, a pinch of salt flakes, and a generous ¾ cup (200 ml) of warm water in a food processor and blend until smooth. Transfer into a bowl, cover with plastic wrap, and refrigerate until required.

Combine the red onion salad ingredients in a bowl.

Preheat a barbecue or grill pan to medium–high.

To prepare the kebabs, thread an onion half onto the end of a skewer. Add 2 pieces of lamb leg, then a piece of fat, and end with another onion half. Repeat to make 8 skewers. Place the skewers on the grill or pan and cook for 3–4 minutes on each side until evenly browned.

Serve the lamb kebabs with the roast chickpea hummus, red onion salad, flatbreads, and garlic yogurt.

Note Roasting chickpeas gives a beautiful nutty flavor. Pre-roasted chickpeas are available at some specialist Middle Eastern grocery stores. You can deep-fry the drained, soaked chickpeas instead of roasting, if preferred.

Roast chickpea hummus
1¼ cups (9 oz/250 g) dried chickpeas, soaked overnight
olive oil
salt flakes
2 garlic cloves, peeled
2½ tablespoons tahini*
⅓ cup (80 ml) lemon juice

Red onion salad
1 small red onion, thinly shaved
handful Italian parsley, leaves picked and torn
handful mint, leaves picked and torn
pinch of sumac*

Lamb kebabs
8 pearl onions, halved crossways
1 lb 2 oz (500 g) boneless lamb leg, diced
7 oz (200 g) lamb tail fat* (or suet or lard), finely diced

flatbread, to serve
garlic yogurt (see page 136), to serve

ICLI KOFTE WITH GARLIC YOGURT AND BROWN BUTTER

I've eaten so many versions of this dish in different parts of the world and everyone claims it as their own, but the one we had in Mardin in southeastern Turkey was right up there with the best of them.

Bring 3 cups (750 ml) of water to a boil in a saucepan over high heat. Combine the bulgur, sabaht baharat, and salt in the bowl of an electric stand mixer. Pour in the boiling water, cover with a lid, and let stand for 30 minutes.

Attach the dough hook to the mixer and knead the bulgur mixture at moderate–high speed for 10–15 minutes, scraping down the sides of the bowl, until the contents resemble a dough consistency—you may need to add a little more hot water if you feel it isn't coming together (see note).

Meanwhile, to make the filling, heat the olive oil in a frying pan over medium heat. Add the lamb and cook for a few minutes, breaking it up with the back of a wooden spoon. Add the onion and stir continuously until the onion is softened. Add the Aleppo pepper and the pistachios. Increase the heat to medium–high and sauté until the onion is translucent and the lamb is evenly browned. Turn out onto a tray and leave to cool.

To make the garlic yogurt, put the yogurt and garlic in a bowl. Add the salt and stir through. Cover with plastic wrap and refrigerate until required.

To make the kofte, put a golf ball–sized amount of the bulgur mixture in your hand and form into a ball. Poke a hole in the ball with your finger, and then make a space for the filling with a tablespoon. Add a teaspoon of the lamb filling and pinch the top to seal the ball. Repeat with the remaining bulgur and filling mixtures to make about 20 balls.

Bring a saucepan of water to a simmer over medium–high heat. Add the kofte and cook for 3–4 minutes until cooked. Remove with a slotted spoon.

Meanwhile, melt the butter in a frying pan over medium–high heat until it starts to foam. Add the red pepper paste, Aleppo pepper, and pistachios and stir. Add the lemon juice and stir to combine. Remove from the heat.

Smear some garlic yogurt on the bottom of each serving plate. Add the icli kofte, spoon on some brown butter, scatter with the sorrel leaves, if using, and serve immediately.

Note It is important to knead the bulgur while it's still warm, since this helps it come together.

Bulgur dough
2¾ cups (1 lb 2 oz/500 g) fine dark bulgur
heaped 1 tablespoon sabaht baharat* (Lebanese 7 spice)
pinch of salt flakes

Lamb and onion filling
1 tablespoon olive oil
7 oz (200 g) ground lamb
1 yellow onion, finely diced
heaped 1 tablespoon Aleppo pepper*
2½ tablespoons slivered pistachios

Garlic yogurt
generous 1 cup (9¼ oz/260 g) Greek yogurt
2 garlic cloves, crushed
pinch of salt flakes

Brown butter
2 tablespoons (1 oz/30 g) butter
heaped 1 tablespoon red pepper paste*
heaped 1 tablespoon Aleppo pepper*
heaped 1 tablespoon pistachios
squeeze of lemon juice

sorrel leaves, to serve (optional)

Cappadocia, Turkey

CORNBREAD AND FENNEL SEED COATED SARDINES

Sardines are a HUGE part of the Turkish diet. Every village has a specialty or secret way of cooking them. Street-side vendors and corner shops all tout them to passing potential customers. Cornbread is another item that's hot property in Turkey, especially in the Black Sea regions where there are as many different styles of cornbread as there are sardine dishes.

This dish is an awesome way of bringing them both together and the cornbread has a great way of mellowing out the sometimes overpowering sardine flavor. So for all you sardine haters out there, give this recipe a try. I promise it won't disappoint!

Combine the crumbled cornbread with the cornmeal, sumac, walnuts, fennel seeds, Aleppo pepper, and thyme leaves on a tray.

Place the sardine fillets in the flour to coat, dip in the beaten egg, then place in the cornbread mixture. Press as much as you can into the sardines to enhance the flavor.

Heat the olive oil and butter in a frying pan over medium heat. Carefully place the sardines in the pan, a few at a time, and cook for 1–2 minutes on each side until golden brown. Transfer to paper towels to soak up the excess oil.

Smear each plate with some garlic yogurt. Place 3 sardines on top, add the sorrel leaves, if using, and lime wedges, and serve.

Notes The cornbread recipe on page 150 makes more than you need here, but it's handy to have on hand and freezes well. Coarsely crumble and store in ziplock bags in the freezer for up to 3 months.

You can use white fish or shrimp instead of sardines.

1 cup (1¾ oz/50 g) crumbled store-bought cornbread (or to make your own, see page 150—see note)
heaped 1 tablespoon cornmeal
1 teaspoon sumac*
¼ cup (1 oz/30 g) coarsely crushed walnuts
1 teaspoon fennel seeds
1 teaspoon Aleppo pepper*
6 thyme stems, leaves picked
12 sardine fillets (about 5½ oz/150 g each), cleaned (see note)
all-purpose flour, for dusting
2 eggs, beaten
1 tablespoon olive oil
2 tablespoons (1 oz/30 g) butter
garlic yogurt (see page 140)
sorrel leaves, to serve (optional)
lime wedges, to serve

Preparation time: 45 minutes • Cooking time: 45 minutes • Serves: 4

SARDINE AND PRESERVED ORANGE RICE PILAF WITH HERBED CRÈME FRAÎCHE

This is a classic Black Sea dish. Every year when sardines are at their peak, every household and local restaurant is cooking sardine pilaf. Of course, everyone seems to have their own version, and no matter who I spoke to, their mom's version was the best. This is my version, which is very close to the traditional dish. I have just tried to make it look a little sharper and the introduction of the preserved orange in the rice adds a nice surprise.

Put the rice in a small saucepan with enough water to cover by ½ inch (1 cm). Bring to a boil, cover with a lid, and cook for 10 minutes until the water has been absorbed and the rice is plump, but still slightly firm.

Heat the olive oil in a frying pan over medium heat. Add the pine nuts and stir until colored, then add the currants, preserved orange, and sabaht baharat. Add the rice and toss through, then add the butter, stir, and remove from the heat. Set aside to cool. Add the dill.

Preheat the oven to 340°F (170°C).

Line a 6 inch (15 cm) Dutch oven or copper pan with parchment paper. Arrange the sardine fillets, with the skin side facing out, around the sides of the pan. Fill the pan with the rice mixture, packing tightly, but stopping about ¼ inch (5 mm) from the top of the pan. Fold over the sardines and place a few more on top to cover the filling. Place a sheet of parchment paper over the sardines and then place a weight on top. Bake in the oven for 30 minutes or until firm.

Meanwhile, to make the herbed crème fraîche, place the herbs, lemon zest, and olive oil in a food processor and purée until smooth.

Add half of the crème fraîche and blend until combined. Transfer to a bowl and fold in the remaining crème fraîche.

Remove the pilaf from the oven and leave to rest for a few minutes, then turn out onto a plate. Dollop a spoonful of the herbed crème fraîche on top and scatter with sorrel leaves, if using. Serve immediately.

Note You can still make this dish even if you don't want to mold it into a cake. Simply grill or pan-fry the sardines and serve alongside the rice mixture. In this case, make sure the rice is cooked for a few more minutes until tender.

½ cup (3¾ oz/110 g) baldo rice (or arborio rice)
2½ tablespoons olive oil
¼ cup (1½ oz/40 g) pine nuts
2½ tablespoons dried currants
2½ tablespoons preserved orange,* peel only, diced
heaped 1 tablespoon sabaht baharat* (Lebanese 7 spice)
1 stick (4 oz/115 g) butter
10 dill sprigs, chopped
1 lb 2 oz (500 g) sardines, filleted and cleaned
sorrel leaves, to serve (optional)

Herbed crème fraîche
small handful Italian parsley
small handful cilantro
small handful mint
small handful dill
zest of 1 lemon
¼ cup (60 ml) olive oil
generous 1 cup (9¼ oz/260 g) crème fraiche

CHICKEN CORNBREAD DUMPLING SOUP

Here is another knockout recipe that I was taught during my travels through Turkey, this one from an old lady who has been cooking the dish for longer than I've been alive. I didn't change it much—just a little polish here and there—but the addition of the dumplings really brought the dish to a new level. This has become a staple in the Delia household. My kids love it, and it's so simple to make. The cornmeal gives the dish a lovely toasted flavor, which to me is the thing that makes it special.

6½ oz (180 g) crumbled store-bought cornbread (or to make your own, see page 150)

6½ oz (180 g) ground chicken (see note)

1 egg white

handful Italian parsley, leaves picked and finely chopped

pinch of red Aleppo pepper*

pinch of salt flakes

7 tablespoons (3½ oz/100 g) butter

1 yellow onion, finely diced

1 corn cob, kernels only

3 tablespoons tomato paste

½ can (7 oz/200 g) cannellini beans, rinsed and drained

⅔ cup (3½ oz/100 g) fine cornmeal (see note)

⅓ cup (80 ml) lemon juice

1 lacinato kale, stems removed

1 tablespoon olive oil

¼ cup (1½ oz/40 g) roasted, peeled, and coarsely crushed hazelnuts

heaped 1 tablespoon Aleppo pepper*

zest of 1 lemon

Combine the cornbread, ground chicken, egg white, parsley, Aleppo pepper, and salt in the bowl of an electric stand mixer. Attach the paddle attachment and mix until combined, then roll the mixture into walnut-sized balls.

Bring a large saucepan of water to a simmer over medium–high heat. Add the dumplings and cook for 3–5 minutes until firm and cooked through. Remove the dumplings from the pan with a slotted spoon and set aside.

Melt 2 tablespoons (1 oz/30 g) of the butter in a large saucepan over medium–high heat. Add the onion and corn and sauté until translucent. Add the tomato paste, beans, and cornmeal, and mix well. Add 8 cups (2 liters) of water, reduce the heat to low, and simmer for 20–25 minutes, stirring occasionally. Add the lemon juice and kale, and season to taste.

Heat the olive oil and remaining butter in a frying pan over medium heat. When the butter starts to foam, add the hazelnuts. Stir through and add the poached dumplings. Add the Aleppo pepper and lemon zest and toss to coat.

Divide the soup between four serving bowls. Add the hazelnut and dumpling mixture and serve immediately.

Notes Use other ground meats to change the flavor.
The cornmeal is used to thicken the soup, but you can leave this out if desired.

TEA-SMOKED DUCK WITH KALE AND HAZELNUT SALAD

This dish sums up the Black Sea region of Turkey for me. Green rolling hills, lots of tea, hazelnuts, and game birds.

You'll need a smoker box and a barbecue to really develop the smoky tea flavor in this recipe.

TURKISH TEA-SMOKED DUCK

Break the hazelnut shells using a mortar and pestle, just enough to be able to remove the nut whole (or as whole as possible). Place the shells in a smoker box with the tea leaves and place the unpeeled hazelnuts on a baking tray.

Preheat the oven to 350°F (180°C).

Roast the hazelnuts for 8 minutes, peel off the skins, and discard, then coarsely crush the hazelnuts and reserve for the kale salad.

Preheat the grill to medium–high.

Place the smoker box on the stove on the highest naked flame. After a couple of minutes it should start smoking. Place the smoker box on the barbecue, put a resting rack on top with the duck breasts on it, cover with a lid, and leave to smoke for 20 minutes.

Remove the duck from the smoker. Heat the butter in a frying pan over medium heat, add the duck, and cook for 3 minutes, skin side down, to render the fat. Turn the duck over and cook for a further 3 minutes or until golden. Transfer to a baking tray and finish in the oven for 4 minutes. Set aside to rest for 5–10 minutes before carving. Slice each breast into thin slices.

CORNBREAD

Preheat the oven to 315°F (160°C). Line a 12 x 8 inch (30 x 20 cm) baking pan with parchment paper.

Using an electric stand mixer fitted with the whisk attachment, beat the yogurt, olive oil, eggs, and 1¾ cups (400 ml) of water until well combined. Add the flour, baking powder, sugar, and salt, and mix on low speed until just combined. With the machine running, slowly add the cornmeal and mix until smooth—the batter will be quite wet. Pour the mixture into the pan and bake for 20 minutes or until a skewer inserted into the center comes out clean. Set aside to cool.

Turkish tea-smoked duck
3¼ cups (9 oz/250 g) hazelnuts in shell
1 cup (2¾ oz/80 g) Turkish tea leaves (or other black tea leaves)
2 x 1 lb 2 oz (200 g) duck breasts, skin on (see note)
2 tablespoons (1 oz/30 g) butter

Cornbread
1⅔ cups (14 oz/400 g) Greek yogurt
¼ cup (60 ml) olive oil
3 eggs
1½ cups (6½ oz/180 g) all-purpose flour
4 teaspoons baking powder
generous ¼ cup (2¼ oz/60 g) sugar
pinch of salt
2¼ cups (11½ oz/330 g) cornmeal
2 tablespoons (1 oz/30 g) butter

Black garlic mayonnaise
3½ oz (100 g) black garlic, peeled (see note)
3 egg yolks
1 egg
heaped 1 tablespoon dijon mustard
heaped 1 tablespoon lemon juice
1¼ cups (300 ml) blended oil (50:50 vegetable oil and olive oil)

Kale and hazelnut salad

3 large lacinato kale leaves, torn
2 garlic cloves
reserved roasted hazelnuts
  (see previous page)
heaped 1 tablespoon Aleppo
  pepper,* plus 1 teaspoon extra
3 tablespoons pomegranate
  molasses*
½ cup (120 ml) olive oil
heaped 1 tablespoon lemon juice
1 French shallot, finely diced
5 basil leaves
1 small handful cilantro, leaves
  picked

Break the cornbread into small chunks to make croutons. Heat the butter in a frying pan over medium heat. When the butter foams, add the cornbread and pan-fry. Set aside until required.

BLACK GARLIC MAYONNAISE

Put the black garlic, egg yolks, egg, mustard, and lemon juice in a food processor and blend until smooth. With the machine running, slowly trickle in the blended oil and continue blending until you have a smooth mayonnaise. Refrigerate until required.

KALE AND HAZELNUT SALAD

Blanch the kale in boiling salted water for 10 seconds, then refresh in iced water. Strain and transfer to paper towels to drain. Set aside until required.

Put the garlic, hazelnuts, and Aleppo pepper in a food processor and blend until well combined. Add the pomegranate molasses, olive oil, and lemon juice and blend until smooth.

To complete the salad, toss the blanched kale leaves with the hazelnut purée, French shallot, extra Aleppo pepper, basil, and cilantro. Season with salt and pepper to taste.

TO SERVE

Place the salad on a plate, add the sliced duck, dollop on the black garlic mayonnaise in the center of the plate, and top with the cornbread croutons. Serve immediately.

Note Black garlic is a type of caramelized garlic. It is available at specialty food stores and online.

Tea-smoked duck with
lacinato kale and hazelnut
salad

MASTIC PUDDING WITH CHOCOLATE SOIL, BLACKBERRY SORBET, AND ROSEMARY PEARLS

All the side streets in Turkey were filled with blackberry bushes growing wild, and all down the Aegean Coast was a herb I didn't expect to find in Turkey—rosemary. The rosemary and the blackberry together with the mastic is a great combination in this dish. If it's your first time using mastic, go easy as it can be overpowering and is an acquired taste.

ROSEMARY PEARLS

To infuse the honey, combine it with the rosemary in a frying pan over medium heat and simmer for 2 minutes. Remove from the heat.

Place 2½ cups (600 ml) of water in a large saucepan and bring to a boil over medium–high heat. Add the tapioca and stir frequently for 14 minutes, until the tapioca is cooked and tender. Strain through a sieve and combine the tapioca with the rosemary-infused honey. Refrigerate overnight, to allow the honey to soak into the tapioca.

CHOCOLATE SOIL

Combine the dry ingredients in a stainless steel bowl. Stir in the melted butter until the mixture looks mealy.

Preheat the oven to 300°F (150°C). Line a baking tray with parchment paper.

Spread the mixture out onto the prepared tray and bake for 15 minutes. Remove from the oven and set aside to cool.

Crumble finely and store in a sealed container.

MASTIC PUDDING

Combine the milk, sugar, rice, and mastic in a saucepan over medium–low heat. Simmer for 15–20 minutes, stirring frequently, until the rice is *al dente*.

Meanwhile, melt the butter in a small saucepan over medium heat. Add the flour and cook, stirring constantly, for 3 minutes or until thickened.

Rosemary pearls
3 tablespoons honey
1 rosemary sprig
⅓ cup (1¾ oz/50 g) tapioca

Chocolate soil
⅔ cup (4½ oz/125 g) sugar
1¼ cups (4½ oz/125 g) almond meal
generous ½ cup (2½ oz/75 g) all-purpose flour
generous ½ cup (1¾ oz/50 g) unsweetened cocoa powder
pinch of salt flakes
3 tablespoons (1½ oz/40 g) butter, melted

Mastic pudding
2 cups (500 ml) milk
generous ¼ cup (2¼ oz/60 g) sugar
2 tablespoons baldo rice (or arborio rice)
½ inch piece (1.5 g) mastic (Arabic gum) (see notes)
3 tablespoons (1½ oz/40 g) butter
6 tablespoons (1¾ oz/50 g) all-purpose flour

Blackberry sorbet
1 lb 2 oz (500 g) blackberries (fresh or frozen, thawed)
3 egg whites
1 cup (7 oz/200 g) sugar

To serve
rosemary flowers, to garnish (optional)

When the rice is cooked, add the flour and butter mixture and continue to stir until the mixture thickens. Reduce the heat to low and continue to cook until the milk mixture starts to slowly boil, then transfer to the bowl of an electric stand mixer. Attach the paddle attachment and beat at high speed until cold. Pour into four serving bowls and refrigerate until set.

BLACKBERRY SORBET

Purée the blackberries in a bowl using a hand-held immersion blender.

Place the blackberry purée and egg whites in the bowl of your stand mixer and whisk at a moderate speed with the whisk attachment for 10 minutes or until the mixture doubles in size.

Meanwhile, make a syrup by combining the sugar and a scant ½ cup (100 ml) of water in a saucepan over medium–high heat, and simmer for approximately 5 minutes to soft ball stage. To test if the syrup is ready, drop a small amount into a shallow bowl of cold water to cool it down. It will form a soft ball. If you have a kitchen thermometer, the syrup will be ready when the temperature reaches about 240°F (115–118°C).

Decrease the speed of the whisk to low and slowly pour in the syrup. Then whisk at a high speed for 3 minutes and continue to whisk until cold. Transfer to a container and freeze.

TO SERVE

Remove the mastic pudding from the fridge. Add a tablespoon of the tapioca pearls over the top and add a thin layer of the chocolate soil. Add a scoop of blackberry sorbet in the middle. Garnish with rosemary flowers, if using, and serve immediately.

Note The blackberry sorbet is really easy to make, since you don't need an ice cream maker. Substitute other berries for a different flavor.

Mastic or Arabic gum (not to be confused with gum Arabic), can be purchased online or at Middle Eastern or Greek grocery stores.

Mastic pudding with chocolate soil, blackberry sorbet, and rosemary pearls

ROSEWATER SUTLAC WITH PISTACHIO CRUMBLE

Rice and milk puddings (called sutlac) are a big part of the Middle Eastern and Turkish menu. I have been eating these for as long as I can remember—some good, some not so good, but none of them have been as delicious as the one I had in the Pontic Mountains around Trabzon. Such a simple dish of sugar, milk, and rice, but when it is cooked with love using only the best ingredients possible it's a recipe for success.

Preheat the oven to 340°F (170°C). Line a baking tray with parchment paper.

Using an electric stand mixer with the paddle attachment, cream the butter, sugar, and pistachio paste for 5 minutes at a moderate speed until pale. Add the flour and pistachios to the bowl, reduce the speed to low, and mix until it just comes together.

Transfer the pistachio mixture onto the prepared baking tray and spread out into an even layer. Place the tray in the oven and bake for 17 minutes or until golden. Remove the shortbread from the oven and set aside until cool enough to handle. Break up into a crumble.

To make the rosewater sutlac, place the milk in a saucepan over medium–high heat. Simmer until the milk has reduced by a third.

In a separate saucepan, cook the rice, adding the milk, a ladleful at a time, stirring continuously, until *al dente*. Add the sugar and rosewater, stir well, and then pour into serving bowls.

Place a mound of pistachio crumble on top of the sutlac. Top with pistachios and mint leaves, and serve either hot or cold.

Notes Pistachio paste is available from specialist Middle Eastern grocery stores. It can also be purchased online.

Use a really fresh cow's or goat's milk for superior flavor.

Pistachio crumble

11 tablespoons (5½ oz/150 g) butter, at room temperature

6 tablespoons (2½ oz/ 75 g) sugar

heaped 1 tablespoon pistachio paste (see note)

2 cups (9 oz/250 g) all-purpose flour

1 cup (4½ oz/125 g) pistachios, plus extra to serve

Rosewater sutlac

4 cups (1 liter) whole milk (see note)

⅓ cup (2¼ oz/60 g) baldo rice (or arborio rice)

⅓ cup (2½ oz/70 g) sugar

½ cup (120 ml) rosewater

small handful mint leaves, to serve

PUMPKIN TURKISH DELIGHT

I love the way the ladies I spent time with in the hills surrounding Fethiye made sucuk pekmez—a sweet made by dipping walnuts or pistachios in syrup to create a sausage. Thickening the molasses with semolina made me think about what other fruits or vegetables I could try using the same technique. The sweetness of pumpkin made me think it would be an easy substitute for the pekmez in the form of a purée, and it turned out to be a great dish. The confectioner's sugar snow really makes it feel like Turkish delight and also represents the snow-capped mountains around Fethiye.

Peel the candied pumpkin, place it in a food processor, and blend until smooth.

Heat the candied pumpkin purée, sugar syrup, and 1¼ cups (300 ml) of water in a heavy-based saucepan, whisking occasionally, until the mixture starts to boil. Add the semolina and stir through, then reduce the temperature to medium–low and cook for 5–8 minutes.

Transfer the mixture into the bowl of an electric stand mixer, attach the paddle attachment, and beat at moderate speed, adding the butter a little at a time, for 10 minutes or until completely cool.

Line a tray with parchment paper and dust with about half of the confectioner's sugar and cornstarch. Add the walnuts to the pumpkin mixture and stir through. Pour the mixture onto the sugared tray and flatten it out evenly. Dust the top with most of the remaining confectioner's sugar and cornstarch to resemble snow and then refrigerate for 3–4 hours to set.

Portion the pumpkin Turkish delight into 1½ inch (4 cm) squares. Dust with any remaining confectioner's sugar and cornstarch and serve.

Notes Sugar syrup is available from specialist confectioners' stores. You can also make your own sugar syrup by mixing equal quantities of sugar and water in a saucepan over low heat until the sugar has dissolved and the mixture thickens.

about 2 cups (1 lb 10 oz/750 g) candied spiced pumpkin or winter squash (see page 61)

scant 2 cups (450 ml) sugar syrup (see note)

1¾ cups (10½ oz/300 g) fine semolina

7 tablespoons (3½ oz/100 g) butter

1¼ cups (5½ oz/150 g) confectioner's sugar

1¼ cups (5½ oz/150 g) cornstarch

½ cup (2¼ oz/60 g) roughly chopped walnuts, toasted

Essaouira

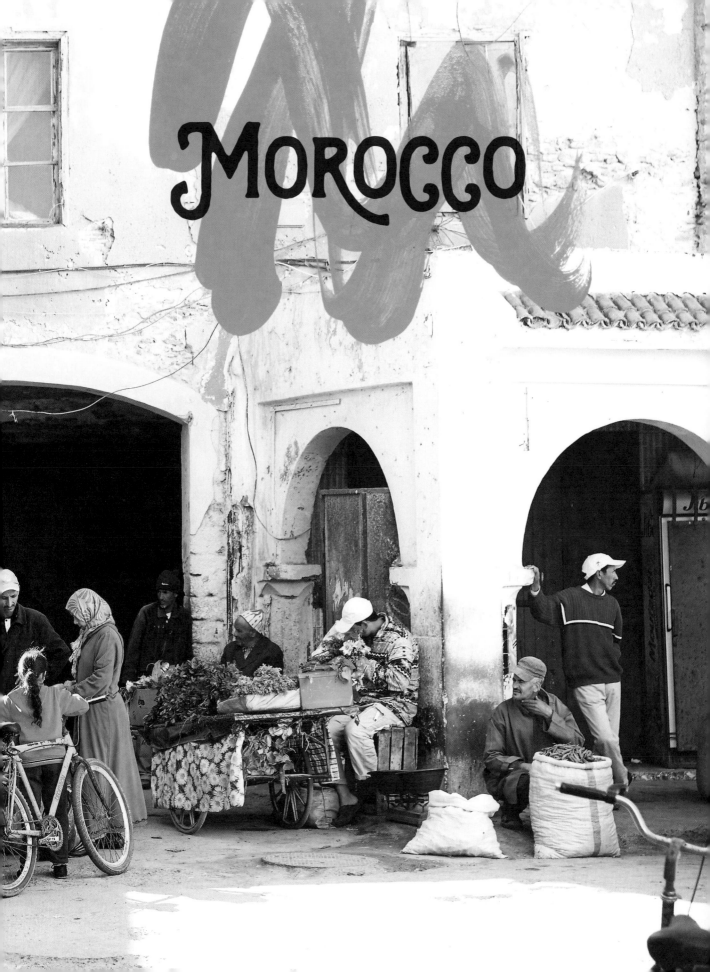

MOROCCO

Magical and mystical. Overflowing with opulence, and a splash of danger and excitement. These were my childhood ideas of Morocco, which came about by watching old movies about the Crusades, Moorish kings and knights, and Bible epics.

On the silver screen I saw a landscape that was hard and unforgiving, yet it had this mesmerizing beauty that transfixed its visitors. I could almost smell the banquets, richly perfumed with the flavors that had been discovered along the medieval spice routes and brought back to the kitchens of the kings. Morocco, to me, has always been liberally sprinkled with wonder and enchantment.

Fez. From hidden alleys of the medina that reveal some beautiful secrets like bissara and sweet mint tea, to wondrous bazaars thick with the aromas of tagine simmering with saffron, to the city's glorious architecture—stunning palaces and riads that have been restored to their former beauty, I've experienced no other place on earth like it. The adrenaline rush you get when you suddenly realize that you are lost in one of the estimated 9000 streets and alleys of the Fez medina is like no other. Many streets don't have a name ... there are no maps and the sun is about to set. You are stuck in an ancient world with no Google or GPS, and filled with a sense of helplessness. To me, that is the most beautiful thing about Fez. You've got no choice but to submit to its ways. You simply have no choice. And then the magic takes hold.

I closed my eyes and started to remember the movies I'd watched as a child. Before I knew it, I was seeing caravan traders walking down the streets, laden with treasures from their long trek through the desert with huge crescent moon–shaped swords, cloths of gold, brightly colored turbans, and jewel-studded sashes; camels and donkeys bustling through the tight alleys loaded with supplies and riches; laughter and music echoing from friends and families reunited after returning home from battling in the Crusades.

It's not that I have some wildly imaginative fantasy about living in a time long forgotten, but it's not that hard to envisage such a world in Morocco. The details and situations may have changed, but Fez, in particular, is still the same. Families are still living in the same homes that have stood here for hundreds of years, donkeys still roam the streets carrying goods to the market or hides to the tannery. Street vendors still work the same corners that have been worked for centuries, and the call to prayer still bellows through the air from medieval minarets.

From Fez it was on through freezing snow to Erfoud and Rissani where I met Berber families who showed me the beauty of the desert and a simpler way of life using only what you need, or what the land can provide. Wind-shaped sand dunes seemed to stretch for miles, changing shape right before your eyes with the setting sun. Oases emerged where life seemed non-existent, filled with people who welcomed me with open arms and dishes ready to fill my empty belly. Date and orange fields filled with the sweet scent of honey, roasting almonds, and freshly baked breads and pastries, and of course the ubiquitous tagines.

Bright green fields filled with poppies, wild thyme, and sunflowers would burst into birdsong with the rising sun. And as I crossed the snow-capped Atlas Mountains into Demnate, the land filled with life and new ingredients: preserved lemons and fruits, and fermented butter from the sheep and cows that roam this beautiful and abundant landscape.

BANG, into the hustle and bustle of Marrakesh, where snake charmers, fortune tellers, meat cooking over coals, and bus-loads of tourists with selfie sticks all cram into the Jemaa el Fna. Forget going to university to get a degree in sales or marketing. The store owners and food vendors here have had thousands of years to perfect their craft and can sell you anything—usually something you would never imagine buying. And if you don't buy it on their first sales pitch they seem to cast a magic spell that ensures you buy it out of guilt. You may as well admit defeat; you have no chance against these masters of persuasion.

Marrakesh is electric, alive, and pumping. It's like watching your favorite band at a live show, drinking too much, then devouring a greasy burger and fries at 3 am on the way home. An amazing night out, no regrets, but you can't quite remember everything that happened.

Morocco will always be a place that excites me. I love the history in the food and the cities, the excitement and chaos I sense all around when walking the streets. You can either come to Morocco and try to change her into what you want or hope she can be, and fail like countless numbers of ruling factions have done over the centuries. Or, you can immerse yourself in what Morocco is and accept her in all her crazy glory. Revel in her successes and look for beauty where it is not so obvious. The soul of the Moroccan people and their country is pure and beautiful. It may not be what you are used to or what you had expected, but if it were wouldn't you be just a little disappointed? ✷

Immerse yourself in what Morocco is and accept her in all her crazy glory.

BISSARA WITH ROASTED GARLIC OIL, SCALLOPS, CARROTS, AND CUMIN

Traditional bissara is a full-on, earthy dish that really sums up the souk. Gutsy and surprising, with just enough spice and olive oil to make it special. But to be honest, it's not really everyone's cup of tea. The fava beans in the traditional recipe can be over-pungent, so I have tamed the recipe and introduced some finesse and sweetness, while trying to keep the essence of the dish intact with a subtle use of spice.

Drain the soaked lima beans and set aside.

Shell the fava beans and discard the large pods. Bring a saucepan of water to a boil and blanch the beans for 1 minute in the boiling water. Remove with a slotted spoon and peel off the skin that encases the beans. Discard the skins. Continue double podding the beans until you have 1 cup (6½ oz/185 g).

Heat the olive oil in a large saucepan over high heat. Add the onion, celery, garlic, and spices, and fry for 4–5 minutes until fragrant. Add the lima beans, cover with 6 cups (1.5 liters) of water, and cook for 15 minutes or until the beans are tender. Remove from the heat and purée with a hand-held immersion blender until smooth. Adjust the seasoning and set aside.

Heat the sugar, lemon juice, and a scant ½ cup (100 ml) of water in a small saucepan over high heat until the sugar has dissolved. Remove from the heat and pour into a large bowl. Cover and refrigerate until cold.

Put the carrots in a saucepan of boiling salted water over high heat and cook for 3 minutes or until just tender. Remove and drain, then refresh in the bowl of cold lemon-sugar water (see note). Season and set aside.

Put the fava beans and drained lentils in a bowl with the cilantro leaves and toss to combine.

Heat a little oil in a small frying pan over high heat, add the almonds and scallops, and cook, turning, for 30–60 seconds until seared on both sides and just cooked through.

Place the fava beans and lentil salad in four shallow bowls, add the carrots, and top with the scallops. Pour on a little of the lima bean purée and drizzle with harissa. Sprinkle with extra paprika and cumin and serve.

Note Refreshing the carrots in the lemon, sugar, and water enhances their natural sweetness. It is a great way to stop the cooking process and retain some texture.

1⅔ cups (10½ oz/300 g) dried lima beans, soaked overnight

1 lb 2 oz (500 g) fresh fava beans

1 tablespoon olive oil, plus extra

1 small yellow onion, diced

1 celery stalk, diced

2 garlic cloves, crushed

1 teaspoon smoked paprika, plus extra to serve

½ teaspoon cumin, plus extra to serve

½ cup (3½ oz/100 g) sugar

scant ½ cup (100 ml) lemon juice

2 handfuls bunched baby carrots, scrubbed, ends trimmed

1 cup (7½ oz/210 g) French (Puy) lentils, cooked

large handful fresh cilantro, leaves picked

handful almonds, roughly chopped

1 lb 2 oz (500 g) small scallops, roe removed

harissa,* to serve

Preparation time: 30 minutes, plus 3 hours marinating and soaking • Cooking time: 1 hour 30 minutes • Serves: 4

RFISSA

Anytime someone teaches me a dish of celebratory and cultural significance I sit up and listen. There was a lot to love about this dish when I first tried it in Morocco—the use of fenugreek and saffron with lentils and harissa created a beautiful sauce for the chicken to be braised in. This is my spin on it.

Place all the marinade ingredients in a shallow bowl and mix well. Add a few tablespoons of water to make a thick paste. Add the chicken and rub the marinade all over. Cover with plastic wrap and place in the fridge for 2–3 hours.

Meanwhile, soak the fenugreek seeds for 2 hours.

Heat about ⅓ cup (80 ml) of the olive oil in a large saucepan over medium heat. Add the onions and cook for 10 minutes until well caramelized. Remove and set aside. Add the marinated chicken to the pan and cook for 8–10 minutes, turning occasionally, until browned on all sides. Return the onions to the pan, add the saffron and remaining ¾ cup (185 ml) of olive oil, and 4 cups (1 liter) of water. Add the fenugreek, lentils, and chickpeas and bring to a boil, then reduce the heat to a simmer and cook for 40 minutes. Remove from the heat.

Remove the chicken from the pan (reserving the sauce), place it in a bowl, and set aside until cool enough to handle, then shred the meat and discard the bones. Add the cilantro and just enough cooking sauce to the shredded chicken to bind. Reserve 1½ cups of the lentils, chickpeas, fenugreek, and sauce for the salad

Preheat the oven to 400°F (200°C). Line a baking tray with parchment paper.

Lay the pastry into long strands, about 4½ x 3¼ inch (12 x 8 cm) lengths. Brush one side with the melted butter.

Place 3 large tablespoons of the shredded chicken mixture at one end of the pastry and roll up. Repeat to make four long parcels.

Place the pastries on the prepared tray, spoon over the sauce left in the pan, and bake for 30 minutes or until golden.

Add the radish, frisee leaves, and eggs to the reserved bowl of sauce, chickpeas, lentils, and fenugreek. Toss together and then dress with some harissa.

Remove the kataifi from the oven and transfer to a serving platter. Spoon over any sauce leftover, and serve with the salad.

Note Kataifi pastry is available at specialty Middle Eastern grocery stores.

Saffron marinated chicken

1 teaspoon ground turmeric
1 tablespoon ground ginger
3 garlic cloves, crushed
pinch of saffron powder
2 chicken leg quarters (about
    14 oz/400 g each)

¼ cup (1¾ oz/50 g) fenugreek seeds
generous 1 cup (265 ml) olive oil
4 yellow onions, thinly sliced
pinch of saffron threads, toasted
½ cup (3½ oz/100 g) green lentils
1 cup (5½ oz/150 g) cooked or
    canned chickpeas
handful cilantro, leaves picked and
    chopped
13 oz (375 g) kataifi pastry (see note)
9 tablespoons (4½ oz/125 g) butter,
    melted
1 baby radish, thinly sliced
handful frisee, leaves picked
4 hard-boiled eggs, sliced
harissa,* to serve

BRAISED CHICKPEA STEW WITH LAMB SHANK, EGGPLANT, AND GRAINS

It's the little things I pick up on my travels that really stick with me. The technique of putting legumes in a cheesecloth bag and cooking it with meat stock was a revelation I discovered in Morocco. It made perfect sense, but I had never seen it before. This way I could cook all my grains and legumes together and they could soak up all the flavor of the dish without being dispersed all through it. Genius!

Soak the chickpeas in cold water for 12 hours or overnight.

Combine the saffron with 3 cups (750 ml) of boiling water.

Preheat the oven to 320°F (165°C).

Mix the remaining spices together in a bowl and season with salt and pepper. Rub the mixture onto the lamb.

Heat the olive oil in a large Dutch oven or tagine pot over medium heat. Add the lamb and brown on all sides. Add the onions, carrots, and half of the dates, then add the tomatoes and saffron water.

Put the soaked chickpeas in a cheesecloth bag, leaving some room for them to expand. Put the freekeh, rice, and bulgur in a second cheesecloth bag, leaving room for expansion in this bag, too. Gently place these in the pot.

Cover the pot with a lid or foil, place in the oven, and cook for 2½ hours or until the meat is tender and falling off the bones.

Meanwhile, place the whole eggplant over a gas flame or grill and cook until the skin is charred and the eggplant is soft. Set aside to cool, then remove the skin and cut the flesh into rough chunks. Set aside.

Make some confit garlic: in a saucepan, heat the garlic cloves with enough olive oil to cover over medium heat for 30 minutes or until they are soft and caramelized. Set aside.

Remove the pot from the oven. Remove the cheesecloth bags and carefully place the contents in a large mixing bowl. Add the eggplant and remaining dates. Season with salt and pepper. Add the parsley and cilantro.

Gently pull the lamb meat from the bones in large chunks. Put the meat into a frying pan with the cooked onions and a ladleful of juices from the pot. Bring to a boil, then add the confit garlic cloves. Season with salt and lemon zest. Add some harissa to taste.

Place the grains in a serving dish, gently spoon over the meat, and serve.

1 cup (7 oz/200 g) dried chickpeas
1 teaspoon ground saffron
2 teaspoons ground turmeric
2 teaspoons smoked paprika
heaped 1 tablespoon ground cumin
2 lb 4 oz (1 kg) cross-cut lamb shank (osso buco)
¼ cup (60 ml) olive oil
10 pearl onions, peeled
2 carrots, peeled and cut into large chunks
10 medjool dates, pitted
4 large ripe tomatoes, grated
1 cup (5½ oz/150 g) freekeh
1¼ cups (7¾ oz/220 g) rice
⅓ cup (1½ oz/40 g) bulgur
1 large eggplant
8 garlic cloves, unpeeled
small handful Italian parsley, leaves picked and chopped
small handful cilantro, leaves picked and chopped
zest of 1 lemon
harissa,* to serve

FOOT OF THE MOUNTAIN COUSCOUS WITH GARDEN VEGETABLES

I remember eating couscous dishes all over Morocco. Lots of flavor and such attention to detail in the presentation of each dish. But for me the biggest let-down was the way it was prepared. The vegetables were always overcooked and collapsed into one. My version pays homage to the beautiful produce I found as I crossed the Atlas Mountains, where the foot of the mountain opened up in full bloom and the air was filled with the smell of wild thyme.

To make the vegetable stock, place all the ingredients and 8 cups (2 liters) of water in a large stockpot over high heat and bring to a boil, then reduce the heat to a simmer and cook for 2 hours. Season with salt and pepper, strain, and set aside.

Preheat the oven to 400°F (200°C).

Place all of the vegetables in a large roasting pan and toss with the olive oil. Add the garlic and rosemary. Cook for about 1½ hours until tender and caramelized.

Meanwhile, blend the thyme and butter together in a small bowl using a wooden spoon, season with salt and pepper, and set aside.

Heat the stock in a saucepan over high heat and add a pinch of saffron threads.

To make the mountain couscous, first rub 1 tablespoon of oil into the couscous to prevent lumps. Transfer to a large bowl with double the volume of hot stock and the salt. Set aside and allow to absorb the liquid completely. Set aside the remaining stock. Add the lemon zest, preserved lemon, almonds, and fresh herbs to the couscous. Rub some of the thyme butter through the couscous to make it fluffy and aerated.

Reheat the remaining stock, add harissa to taste, then pour into a large serving jug.

Put the vegetables on a large serving plate and drizzle over some of the harissa stock and the remaining thyme butter. Scatter over the fennel fronds and serve with the remaining sauce and the couscous.

Vegetable stock

2 large fennel bulbs, halved
2 large yellow onions, halved
2 leeks, trimmed and halved
4 large tomatoes, halved
large pinch of saffron threads
handful herbs (such as rosemary, bay leaf, thyme)

3 small onions
3 small zucchinis (or zucchini flowers), cut lengthways
2 lb (900 g) kabocha squash, cut into thin wedges
2 small fennel bulbs, halved, fronds reserved
½ small cabbage, quartered
8 baby potatoes
8 small purple potatoes (optional)
8 bunched baby carrots, scrubbed
½ cup (120 ml) olive oil, plus 1 tablespoon extra for the couscous
6 garlic cloves
4 rosemary sprigs
handful fresh thyme, leaves picked
9 tablespoons (4½ oz/125 g) butter, softened
pinch of saffron threads
3 cups (1 lb 2 oz/500 g) couscous
pinch of salt
zest of 1 lemon
heaped 1 tablespoon chopped preserved lemon peel
1 cup (3¼ oz/95 g) chopped almonds, toasted
handful fresh herbs (such as cilantro or mint), chopped
2½ tablespoons harissa*

SARDINE KEFTA WITH FRESH CHERMOULA SALAD

If sardines aren't really your thing (I get it that they can be a bit full on), that doesn't mean you should just black-list them for the rest of your days. They are a great little fish, sustainable, and have a great flavor. The flavor intensity just needs to be turned down from a 10 to a 3, and this recipe does just that. The introduction of carrot, adding heaps of sweetness, and some choice spicing really mellows out the fishy sardine flavor. This is a really easy and safe way to start back on the sardine dating scene. Come on. Give it a try.

Mix the sardines and fish with the diced garlic, breadcrumbs, chili, mint, spices, parsley, and lemon zest to bind. Roll into golf ball–sized balls and set aside.

Heat the olive oil in a Dutch oven or tagine pot over medium heat. Place the kefta in the pot and brown for a few minutes on all sides, turning as required. Remove the kefta and set aside. Place the banana shallots and garlic slices in the pot and cook over low heat for a few minutes until golden and softened.

Place the remaining ingredients in the pot, along with the kefta. Pour in enough saffron water to cover. Place over a gentle heat, cover with a lid, and cook for about 20 minutes, until the sauce has thickened and the kefta are cooked through.

To make the chermoula paste, blend all the ingredients together in a food processor until smooth. Store in an airtight container in the fridge until ready to use.

To make the salad, mix the herbs and olive oil into the chermoula in a serving bowl.

Serve the tagine in the middle of the table for people to help themselves with pan-fried potato breads (see page 182) and the fresh chermoula salad on the side.

Note Ask your fishmonger to grind the fish. If you're not a fan of sardines, substitute with any white fish, since this dish is really simple and delicious.

Banana shallots are mild, elongated shallots. If you can't find them, use French shallots instead.

Chermoula paste may be stored in the fridge for 2 weeks.

7 oz (200 g) fresh sardine fillets, ground (see note)
10½ oz (300 g) white fish fillets, ground (see note)
2 garlic cloves, finely diced
½ cup (2 oz/55 g) dry breadcrumbs
1 red bird's eye chili, seeded and diced
1 teaspoon dried mint
1 teaspoon ground turmeric
1 teaspoon sweet paprika
small handful Italian parsley, leaves picked and chopped
zest of 1 lemon
2½ tablespoons olive oil
6 whole banana shallots, peeled and halved (see note)
6 garlic cloves, sliced
2 tomatoes, grated
2 carrots, grated
4 cups (1 liter) saffron water*

Chermoula paste
1 garlic bulb
4 French shallots
¼ cup (¾ oz/20 g) coriander seeds
¼ cup (¾ oz/20 g) cumin seeds
1 preserved lemon, peel only
½ cup (120 ml) olive oil

Fresh chermoula salad
handful Italian parsley, leaves picked
handful cilantro, leaves picked
handful mint, leaves picked
⅓ cup (80 ml) olive oil
heaped 1 tablespoon chermoula paste (see above)

PAN-FRIED POTATO BREADS

Shut the gates and lock the door, because when people start to smell the aromas from cooking these little bundles of joy you will have lines out the front door ready to get their serving. I was over-eating either heavy bread or potato with every dish when I was traveling through Morocco, so it got me thinking—what if I could keep the integrity of the cuisine, but raise the bread up to make it a hero of the dish, not just a sauce mopper or filler? This light, fluffy potato bread was the result.

Heat the milk and sugar in a small saucepan over low heat until warm. Add the yeast, remove from the heat, and allow to sit for 15 minutes.

Meanwhile, put the potatoes in a large saucepan, cover with cold water, and bring to a boil over high heat, then cook for 10 minutes or until tender. Drain and pass through a food mill or sieve until very smooth and then place in a large bowl. Add the eggs, flour, and extra virgin olive oil and mix well to combine. Add the yeast mixture and knead well, adding more flour if necessary to keep the batter from becoming too sticky. Cover with a dish towel and set aside in a warm place for 1 hour or until doubled in size. Punch down the dough and divide into 12 portions.

Lightly flour your work surface and roll each piece of dough out to about ¾ inch (2 cm) thickness.

Heat 1 tablespoon of the olive oil in a large heavy-based frying pan over high heat. Working in batches, fry the dough for about 5 minutes until golden brown, turning over halfway through. Remove from the pan and transfer onto a plate lined with paper towel to soak up the excess oil. Repeat with the remaining oil and dough.

Notes Make sure the potatoes are cooked all the way through since you don't want any lumps.

You can sprinkle the dough with semolina for extra texture just before cooking in the pan.

This is a versatile bread that goes well with many Moroccan dishes; for example, it's delicious served with the sardine kefta with fresh chermoula salad on page 181.

½ cup (120 ml) milk

2 tablespoons sugar

1 envelope (¼ oz/7 g) active dry yeast

1 lb 2 oz (500 g) roasting potatoes (russet or Idaho are good), peeled and cut into chunks

2 eggs

4¼ cups (1 lb 2½ oz/525 g) all-purpose flour, plus extra for dusting

¼ cup (60 ml) extra-virgin olive oil

½ cup (120 ml) olive oil, for frying

The rear wall of El Badi Palace, Marrakesh

LAMB SHOULDER WITH POTATO AND EGGPLANT TAGINE

You can't beat eating a traditional tagine in the Sahara. Even if the dish isn't the most mind-blowing, the atmosphere of eating under the stars in the desert with Berbers is an experience that is hard to match. Here's my rendition of a traditional Moroccan tagine, without the magical setting admittedly, but packed full of beauty in the flavors of the dish.

Mix together the cumin, paprika, and salt in a bowl and then rub generously all over the lamb pieces.

Heat the olive oil in a heavy-based frying pan over high heat, add the lamb, and cook for 15 minutes, turning occasionally, until browned on all sides. Remove and set aside.

Add the onions to the pan and sauté until softened and starting to color. Add the garlic and cook, stirring frequently, for a minute until fragrant. Transfer the onion mixture into a tagine pot or Dutch oven and place a layer of potatoes on top. Add the meat and top with the eggplant wedges. Add the tomatoes.

Dissolve the saffron in 4 cups (1 liter) of water and then pour into the pot to cover the lamb. Nestle in the dates. Cover with a lid, bring to a boil over high heat, reduce the heat to a simmer, and cook for 45 minutes or until the meat is tender.

Meanwhile, make the gremolata. Heat the olive oil and butter in a small frying pan over high heat, add the bread chunks, and cook, turning regularly, until the bread is crunchy and browned all over. Remove from the heat, add the walnuts, dates, ginger, parsley, and lemon zest and stir together. Check and adjust the seasoning.

Serve the tagine with a generous amount of gremolata over the top and a drizzle of harissa.

¼ cup (1 oz/30 g) ground cumin

2½ tablespoons sweet paprika

heaped 1 tablespoon salt

2 lb 4 oz (1 kg) boneless lamb shoulder, cubed

2½ tablespoons olive oil

2 large yellow onions, sliced

6 garlic cloves, crushed

3 potatoes, peeled and sliced

3 Lebanese (long thin) eggplants, cut into large wedges

2 tomatoes, grated

pinch of saffron threads

6 medjool dates, pitted

Gremolata

2 tablespoons olive oil

1½ tablespoons (¾ oz/20 g) butter

a small roll of good-quality artisan bread, broken into chunks

generous 1 cup (4 oz/115 g) walnuts, toasted

about 7 pitted medjool dates (5½ oz/150 g), roughly diced

heaped 1 tablespoon freshly grated ginger

handful Italian parsley, chopped

zest of 1 lemon

harissa,* to serve

Preparation time: 20 minutes • Cooking time: 50 minutes • Serves: 8

HARIRA SOUP WITH PAN-FRIED CHICKEN DUMPLINGS AND FAVA BEAN SALAD

This was a really hard dish to draw inspiration from. I really love it just the way it is. Hearty, and full of flavor and love. It's a big hug from Mom when you haven't seen her in a while, and how can you get better than that? So I just tried to pick up on the things that made the dish special when I tasted it in Marrakesh, and have tried to bring them to life in a lighter way. The best thing that came out of the recipe is the chicken dumpling—mega tasty and something great to make with the kids.

Heat the olive oil in a large saucepan over high heat, add the garlic and onions, and cook for about 5 minutes to soften without coloring. Add the spices, rice, and lentils, stirring to coat, and cook for 2 minutes, then add the tomatoes and 5 cups (1.25 liters) of water. Season with sea salt and freshly ground black pepper. Bring to a boil then simmer for 40 minutes. Add the parsley, remove from the heat, and then purée until smooth using a hand-held immersion blender.

To make the dumplings, heat 1 tablespoon of the olive oil in a frying pan over high heat, add the celery, garlic shoots, and onion and sauté for 1–2 minutes until softened. Remove from the heat, transfer to a large mixing bowl, and set aside to cool.

Add the chives, ginger, and ground chicken to the bowl and mix together well. Place a teaspoon of the chicken mixture in the middle of a gyoza wrapper, fold in half, brush the edge with water, and pleat the pastry to seal the edge. Repeat with the remaining filling and wrappers.

Heat the remaining oil in a large shallow frying pan over medium heat. Add the gyoza and fry on one side for 5 minutes until the pastry is golden. Reduce the heat to low, add the stock, cover with a lid, and steam for about 4 minutes until the liquid has evaporated and the filling is cooked. Remove from the heat and keep warm.

Mix the fava bean salad ingredients together in a small bowl.

To serve, place 3 gyoza in the middle of each serving bowl, pour over some harira, and dress the top of the dumplings with some of the fava bean salad. Serve with the remaining fava bean salad alongside.

Notes Gyoza wrappers are available from East Asian supermarkets.

Harira soup

2½ tablespoons olive oil
2 garlic cloves, chopped
2 large red onions, chopped
1 teaspoon ground turmeric
1 teaspoon ground cumin
1 teaspoon cayenne pepper
pinch of saffron threads
½ teaspoon ground ginger
1 cinnamon stick
½ cup (3¾ oz/110 g) rice
1 cup (7½ oz/215 g) green lentils
14 oz (400 g) canned diced
    tomatoes
2½ tablespoons chopped Italian
    parsley

Chicken dumplings

¼ cup (60 ml) olive oil
1 celery stalk, diced
4 garlic shoots
½ yellow onion, finely diced
2½ tablespoons finely chopped
    chives
heaped 1 tablespoon freshly grated
    ginger
5½ oz (150 g) ground chicken thigh
24 gyoza wrappers (see note)
1 cup (250 ml) chicken stock

Fava bean salad

1 cup (6½ oz/185 g) fava beans,
    podded and peeled
1 preserved lemon, peel only,
    finely diced
2 French shallots, thinly sliced
handful cilantro, leaves picked

WAGYU BEEF WITH ROASTED CAULIFLOWER HUMMUS AND AMLOU DRESSING

I remember when I was first exposed to argan oil several years ago. I have to say I wasn't too impressed. A lot of Morocco's argan oil is produced in a very primitive way, where the quality of the oil is compromised and a very sub-par product is the end result.

I can't tell you how excited I was to finally experience quality argan oil at its best. It was a whole new experience and has started me on a journey exploring the flavor possibilities for this truly beautiful product. Be careful to use the right oil.

Preheat the oven to 400°F (200°C). Line a baking tray with parchment paper.

Put the cauliflower florets on the prepared tray and roast for 40 minutes or until soft and lightly colored. Remove from the oven and set aside to cool (see note).

Season the beef with freshly ground black pepper and sea salt. Sear for 10 minutes on all sides in a heavy-based frying pan over high heat. Add the rosemary sprig to the pan and baste the beef with the pan juices. Transfer to the oven and cook for 4 minutes. Remove from the oven and set aside to rest.

Put the cauliflower in a food processor with the cream and blend until smooth. Add the chickpeas, garlic, tahini, and lemon juice and whiz until smooth. Check and adjust the seasoning.

To make the amlou dressing, mix together the argan oil, almonds, honey, and sherry vinegar in a small bowl.

In a separate bowl, mix the Aleppo pepper, shallots, and chives with a couple of spoonfuls of the amlou.

Thinly slice the beef. Toss with some amlou dressing, radishes, and the salad leaves.

Place the roasted cauliflower hummus on a plate, top with the wagyu beef and salad, drizzle with any remaining dressing, and serve.

Note Roasting the cauliflower brings out the natural sweetness and gives the hummus a delicious flavor.

1 cauliflower, broken into florets
1 lb 2 oz (500 g) wagyu beef top round steak
1 rosemary sprig
½ cup (120 ml) light cream
14 oz (400 g) can chickpeas, rinsed and drained
3 garlic cloves
¼ cup (2¼ oz/60 g) tahini*
2½ tablespoons lemon juice
½ cup (120 ml) argan oil*
1 cup (5½ oz/150 g) almonds, roasted
2½ tablespoons honey
¼ cup (60 ml) sherry vinegar
1 teaspoon Aleppo pepper*
2 French shallots, diced
heaped 1 tablespoon finely chopped chives
small radishes, watercress, and sorrel leaves, to serve

VEAL SHANK AND SAFFRON WITH CARROT AND PRESERVED ORANGE PURÉE

This was one of the tastiest dishes I ate while in Morocco—soft meat, big saffron and caramelized onion flavors, and that little hint of sweet and salty preserved citrus right at the end. This is a great wintry recipe you will want to sit down to with some good bread, a big bottle of red, and some friends or family to help you finish off all the sauce at the bottom of the dish.

Put the veal in a bowl, add the saffron, cumin, and 1 tablespoon of the olive oil, and combine to completely cover the meat. Season with salt and pepper.

Heat another tablespoon of the oil in a tagine pot or Dutch oven over medium heat, add the veal, and cook for a few minutes on each side to brown. Remove the meat from the pan, add the remaining oil, and sauté the onions, garlic, and preserved lemon for a few minutes until softened. Deglaze the pan with the wine, then add the stock and bring to a boil. Return the meat to the pan, reduce the heat to low, and cook for 1½ hours until the meat falls away from the bones.

Meanwhile, put the carrots, onions, split peas, and stock in a saucepan over medium–high heat and cook for 40 minutes until tender. Transfer into a food processor, add the preserved orange peel and ginger, and purée until smooth. Check and adjust the seasoning as required. Set aside.

To serve, divide the veal between the serving plates and sprinkle with the almonds, parsley, and lemon zest. Place the purée in a separate bowl.

Note You can also cook this dish in a pressure cooker. The meat will cook in about half the time.

Veal shank and saffron

4 lb 8 oz (2 kg) cut veal shanks
pinch of saffron threads
1 teaspoon saffron powder
heaped 1 tablespoon ground cumin
¼ cup (60 ml) olive oil
6 red onions, thinly sliced
4 garlic cloves
2 preserved lemon peel strips
1 cup (250 ml) dry white wine
2 cups (500 ml) chicken stock

Carrot and preserved orange purée

2 lb 4 oz (1 kg) carrots, peeled
2 yellow onions, quartered
1¼ cups (9 oz/250 g) dried split peas
2 cups (500 ml) chicken stock
1 preserved orange,* peel only
1½ inch (4 cm) piece fresh ginger

handful almonds, roughly chopped,
   to serve
heaped 1 tablespoon chopped
   Italian parsley leaves, to serve
zest of 1 lemon, to serve

PRESERVED LEMON AND DESERT VEGETABLE MEDFOUNA

Delicious fillings wrapped in bread, what's not to love? Medfouna is a traditional Moroccan dish made with lamb and beef, and the ones I ate in Morocco were winners on all levels. Here's my version using a vegetable filling instead of meat.

Preheat the oven to 200°F (100°C). Line a baking tray with parchment paper.

Remove the pith and pulp from the preserved lemons and discard. Place the skins flat on the prepared tray and bake for 3 hours or until dried out. Remove from the oven and leave to cool, then whiz in a food processor or spice grinder to make a powder. Set aside until ready to serve.

Mix the sugar and yeast in a jug with 1 cup (250 ml) of lukewarm water and allow to sit for 10 minutes until the yeast bubbles.

Mix the flours and salt together in a bowl, by hand. Add the activated yeast and water with the milk. Knead until soft and smooth. Cover with a dish towel and leave to rest for 20 minutes.

Knead the dough for 10 minutes, adding extra flour if the mixture is sticky. Divide the dough into 4 portions. Cover and allow to rise until almost doubled.

Preheat the oven to 400°F (200°C).

To make the vegetable filling, heat the olive oil in a heavy-based frying pan over medium–high heat. Add the onions and cook for about 20 minutes, until caramelized. Remove from the heat.

Mix all the vegetable filling ingredients together, including the caramelized onion, in a bowl. Check the seasoning and adjust as necessary.

When the dough is ready, sprinkle your work surface with a mixture of the coarse semolina, poppyseeds, and crushed coriander seeds.

Divide each dough portion in half to make 8 portions, then roll out each piece of dough on the seeds, into 2 thin circles about the size of a side plate, with one piece slightly larger than the other. Divide the filling into four and put a filling portion on a larger dough piece, leaving some room around the edge. Place a smaller dough piece on top, fold over and seal the edges. Repeat with the remaining dough pieces and filling.

Heat some olive oil in a frying pan over high heat and cook, in batches, for 3 minutes on each side. Remove from the heat, place on the baking tray, and bake for 10 minutes until golden. Sprinkle the medfouna with 1 tablespoon of the preserved lemon powder and serve.

4 preserved lemons

1 teaspoon sugar

1 envelope (¼ oz/7 g) active dry yeast

2⅓ cups (10½ oz/300 g) all-purpose flour, plus extra for dusting

1¼ cups (5½ oz/150 g) wholewheat flour

1 teaspoon salt

⅓ cup (80 ml) milk

2½ tablespoons coarse semolina

2½ tablespoons poppyseeds

2½ tablespoons crushed coriander seeds

olive oil, for frying

Vegetable filling

scant ½ cup (100 ml) olive oil

6 onions, thinly sliced

2 tomatoes, grated

heaped 1 tablespoon finely diced preserved lemon peel

2 cups (1 lb/450 g) fresh ricotta cheese

2 zucchinis, grated

heaped 1 tablespoon smoked paprika

handful cilantro, leaves picked and roughly chopped

handful Italian parsley, leaves picked and roughly chopped

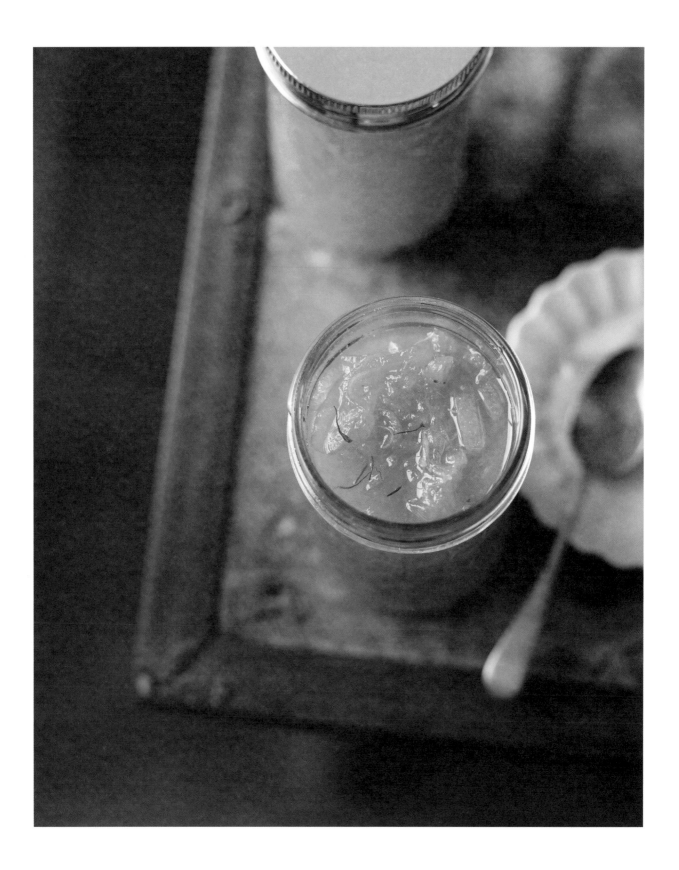

CLEMENTINE AND SAFFRON MARMALADE

Clementine oranges are so undervalued. They should be eaten by the kilogram when in season, and this is one of the best recipes I know of to preserve them for the months when you can't find them and you crave them! The mix of saffron with the sweet tang of the clementine is pure gold.

Remove the peel from the clementines and thinly slice the peel. Place the fruit segments, along with the peel, in a large glass bowl, add 8 cups (2 liters) of water and the lemon juice, cover, and set aside to soak overnight.

Pour the clementines and soaking liquid into a large stockpot and bring to a boil over high heat. Add the sugar and stir to dissolve. Add the saffron. Return to a boil and continue to cook for about 40 minutes, until the marmalade jells when tested on a cold plate. To test that it has set, place a small plate in the freezer. Place a drop of marmalade on the saucer and return to the freezer for 1 minute. Test by running your finger through the marmalade. If it wrinkles and forms a skin, it is ready. Pour the marmalade into sterilized jars, allow to cool, and seal. Serve on toast as part of a breakfast feast.

Note Clementine and saffron marmalade can be processed for longer term storage, if desired (follow the USDA guide to home canning). Otherwise, store in the fridge for up to 1 month or the freezer for up to a year.

2 lb 4 oz (1 kg) clementines
   (or mandarins)
2½ tablespoons lemon juice
5½ cups (2 lb 7 oz/1.1 kg) sugar
pinch of saffron threads

ORANGE GROVE BEGHRIR WITH ORANGE BLOSSOM YOGURT

Traditional beghrir are a kind of "crumpcake"—a mix between a crumpet and a pancake. I loved it when I tasted it in Morocco. What I did when I came home was take the best bit of the Beghrir, which was the crunchy semolina base, and brought it to this recipe. It worked a treat and now this is a dish you will find in the Delia house every Sunday morning for breakfast. They are so easy to make and, let me tell you, once you have cooked them once, it won't be your last time.

Mix the yogurt with the orange blossom water in a small bowl. Line a fine mesh sieve with cheesecloth and place over a bowl. Place the yogurt in the cheesecloth to drain for a few hours until thickened.

Put the yeast and sugar in a bowl, then whisk in 1¼ cups (300 ml) of lukewarm water. Set aside in a warm spot for 15 minutes or until frothy.

Put the flour, semolina, cream of tartar, salt, and milk in the bowl of an electric stand mixer. Add the activated yeast and mix with the dough hook at low speed for about 8 minutes until a dough forms. Cover with a dish towel and leave the mixture to proof for 1 hour or until it starts to form bubbles. Add the baking soda and mix for a further 2 minutes at a moderate speed to incorporate.

To cook the beghrir, oil four egg rings with a pastry brush and place in a frying pan over medium heat. Sprinkle some semolina in each ring. Pour the beghrir mixture into the egg rings, cook on one side for about 5 minutes, until holes form on the surface and the top has begun to set. Flip over and cook on the other side for 1–2 minutes more. Repeat with the remaining batter to make 8 beghrir. (You can do this freehand as well.)

Serve with clementine marmalade and the orange blossom yogurt.

Notes The semolina gives added texture to the base of the beghrir when you are cooking them. You can use a skewer to aid the holes forming in the tops of the beghrir, before turning to cook on the other side.

2 cups (1 lb 2 oz/500 g) Greek yogurt

1–2 tablespoons orange blossom water*

1 envelope (¼ oz/7 g) active dry yeast

½ teaspoon superfine sugar

2 cups (9 oz/250 g) all-purpose flour

¾ cup (4½ oz/125 g) coarse semolina, plus extra for dusting (see note)

½ teaspoon cream of tartar

1 teaspoon salt

generous ¾ cup (200 ml) lukewarm milk

½ teaspoon baking soda

1 tablespoon olive oil

clementine marmalade (see page 199), to serve

MINT AND APPLE PASTILLA WITH DATE AND RAS EL HANOUT ICE CREAM

I don't know anyone who doesn't love an apple pie. This recipe has everything you need in an apple pie—gooey apple filling, caramelized apple flavors, crispy pastry, and just enough spice to wake you up and make it interesting.

I really wanted to pay homage to the original pastille. It is such a wonderful dish that is loved by so many people. I think this dish has done that. It's not pretending to be authentic, but what it has is the soul and complexity of texture that the original has.

But the real winner of this dish is the ice cream! Do yourself a favor and make a big batch of it because once you taste it you won't want to stop eating it. It is one of the best ice creams I have ever made.

DATE AND RAS EL HANOUT ICE CREAM

Put the sugar and 1 cup (250 ml) of water in a saucepan over low heat and stir gently to dissolve. Remove from the heat, add the dates, and purée until smooth using a hand-held immersion blender. Set aside to cool.

Beat the egg yolks using an electric stand mixer with the whisk attachment on moderate–high speed until thick and pale. Add to the cooled date purée.

Whip the cream in a separate bowl to soft peaks with the whisk attachment. Fold the date purée and egg yolk mixture into the cream. Season with ras el hanout to taste, transfer to a container, and freeze for 2–3 hours.

MINT CRÈME

Heat the milk in a small saucepan over high heat, remove from the heat, add the mint leaves, and set aside for 10 minutes to infuse. Pour the mixture through a sieve, discarding the mint leaves, and return the infused milk to the pan. Add the remaining ingredients to the pan and whisk over medium–low heat for 15 minutes until thick. Place the mixture in a pastry bag and set aside.

APPLE PASTILLA

Heat 3 tablespoons (1½ oz/45 g) of the butter in a frying pan over medium heat and sprinkle in the superfine sugar. Stir until dissolved, then reduce the heat to low, add the apples, and cook for about 20 minutes, turning occasionally, until soft and burnished in color. Remove from the heat and set aside.

Date and ras el hanout ice cream

scant 1 cup (6 oz/175 g) sugar
12 medjool dates, pitted
8 egg yolks
4 cups (1 liter) whipping cream
2½ tablespoons ras el hanout*

Mint crème

2¾ cups (670 ml) milk
large handful mint, leaves picked
1 vanilla bean, split and seeds
    scraped
¼ cup (1 oz/30 g) cornstarch
⅓ cup (2¼ oz/60 g) semolina
¾ cup (5½ oz/150 g) sugar
2 eggs
few drops mint essence

Apple pastilla

1½ sticks (6 oz/170 g) butter
½ cup (3¾ oz/110 g) superfine sugar
3 golden delicious apples, peeled,
    cored, and cut into wedges
¾ cup (3½ oz/100 g) almonds,
    toasted and roughly chopped
1 cup (3½ oz/100 g) confectioner's
    sugar, plus extra for dusting
heaped 1 tablespoon ground
    cinnamon
8 sheets filo pastry (see note)
mint leaves, to serve

Preheat the oven to 400°F (200°C). Line a baking tray with parchment paper. Melt the remaining 9 tablespoons (4½ oz/125 g) of butter in the microwave.

Mix the almonds, confectioner's sugar, and cinnamon together in a bowl. Set aside.

Take a sheet of filo pastry and brush with butter. Sprinkle with some of the almond mixture and top with another sheet of filo. Using a 3½ inch (9 cm) round cutter, cut out eight circles. Repeat this step with the remaining pastry and almond mixture. You will have 32 circles.

Place four 3½ inch (9 cm) ring molds (see note) on the prepared baking tray.

Place one circle of filo in the bottom of each mold, brush with melted butter, and sprinkle with some of the almond mixture. Overlap four circles in a petal pattern around the inside of each mold to cover the sides, so the pastry evenly overhangs the edges, and gently brush with butter. Place another circle of filo in each mold to hold the four circles of pastry in position. Place some apple filling in each mold.

Pipe in enough mint crème to cover. Place one round of filo on top of each, brush with butter, and sprinkle with the almond mixture. Fold over the pastry petals neatly. Brush the top with melted butter, sprinkle with almond mixture, and top with the last filo circle. Bake in the oven for 30 minutes or until the pastry is brown and crisp.

Remove the pastilla from the oven and remove the ring molds. Rest for 5 minutes then invert onto a plate.

TO SERVE

Dust the apple pastilla with confectioner's sugar and place on four individual plates. Add a scoop of date and ras el hanout ice cream and serve.

Note It is important to prevent the filo pastry from drying out. Keep it covered with a clean cloth until you need it. Brush with plenty of melted butter to keep it pliable. If you don't have ring molds, you can use ramekins.

Mint and apple pastilla
with date and ras el
hanout ice cream

CHOCOLATE AND PISTACHIO M'HENCHA

Bringing together the techniques and flavors of the old and new schools— this dish was a meld of the refined Moroccan–French food I saw at the Selman hotel in Marrakesh and the old-school beauty of a traditional m'hencha (a type of pastry cake). The flavor combination that resulted was something that I am definitely going to put on the menu at Maha. I love the way the ginger comes into play with this dish.

Put the chocolate, pistachios, palm sugar, saffron, ginger, and 2 tablespoons (1 oz/30 g) of the melted butter in a food processor and blend until finely ground (see note).

Preheat the oven to 350°F (180°C). Line a baking tray with parchment paper.

Open out the sheets of filo, keeping them in a pile so they don't dry out. Take 1 sheet and brush with a little melted butter.

Take lumps of the chocolate nut paste and roll into fingers. Place them end to end on the top sheet of filo, then roll the top sheet around the filling into a roll the thickness of your thumb, tucking in the ends. Repeat with the other filo sheets until the filling is used up.

Press the filo rolls inwards from both ends like an accordion, to relax the pastry, before coiling it to make 8 small coils. Arrange these on the prepared tray.

Brush some extra butter over the pastry, then bake for 30 minutes or until golden and crisp.

Notes The filling can be made 1 day ahead of time and refrigerated until required.

You can substitute different flavors for the filling, such as almonds, hazelnuts, and walnuts.

Palm sugar usually comes in cakes and can be purchased from East Asian grocery stores. Alternatively, you can use ¾ cup (4½ oz/125 g) granulated palm sugar.

7 oz (200 g) dark chocolate
2¾ cups (12 oz/350 g) pistachios
4½ oz (125 g) palm sugar (see note)
pinch of saffron powder
heaped 1 tablespoon ground ginger
1 stick (4 oz/115 g) butter, melted
8 sheets filo pastry

DATE, ORANGE, AND OLIVE OIL CAKE WITH SALTED WHITE CHOCOLATE ICE CREAM

The palm groves of Morocco are breathtaking. Miles of trees producing some of the most high quality dates I have ever seen. On my travels, some Bedouin men showed me that if you warm dates in olive oil before placing them in a tagine it helps bring out the flavor of the caramel in the date. This got me thinking, and led to this recipe.

SALTED WHITE CHOCOLATE ICE CREAM

Put the sugar and 1 cup (250 ml) of water in a saucepan over low heat to dissolve. Add the white chocolate and mix until smooth. Remove from the heat and set aside to cool.

Using an electric stand mixer with a paddle attachment, beat the egg yolks at moderate–high speed until thick and pale, then add to the cooled chocolate.

Whip the cream to stiff peaks in the mixer with the whisk attachment.

Fold the chocolate into the cream using a spatula. Season with salt to taste.

Pour the mixture into a container and freeze for 2–3 hours.

DATE, ORANGE AND OLIVE OIL CAKE

Mix the breadcrumbs, almond meal, a generous 1 cup (7¾ oz/220 g) of the sugar, the ras el hanout, and baking powder together in a bowl.

Whisk the eggs together in a bowl with the olive oil. Add the zests and stir to combine. Fold the egg mixture into the breadcrumb mixture until just combined.

Line an 8¼ x 4¼ inch (21 x 11 cm) loaf pan with parchment paper and pour in the mixture. Place the cake in a cold oven and turn on to 340°F (170°C). Bake for 45 minutes or until the cake is golden, and cooked when tested with a skewer.

Put the remaining ingredients with the remaining sugar (about ¼ cup/1¾ oz/ 50 g) in a saucepan over high heat. Bring to a boil then reduce the heat and simmer for a few minutes. Remove from the heat.

Remove the cake from the oven and pierce all over with a wooden skewer. Drizzle over the spiced syrup and leave for a few minutes to soak up the syrup.

TO SERVE

Remove the salted white chocolate ice cream from the freezer and leave to soften slightly. Cut the cake into slices and serve warm or cold with the ice cream.

Note You can use different shaped pans instead of the loaf pan. If so, you may need to adjust the cooking time.

Salted white chocolate ice cream

generous ¾ cup (6 oz/175 g) superfine sugar

1 lb 2 oz (500 g) white chocolate melting wafers (or chocolate chips)

8 egg yolks

4 cups (1 liter) whipping cream

pinch of sea salt

Date, orange, and olive oil cake

½ cup (1¾ oz/50 g) panko breadcrumbs

1⅓ cups (6½ oz/180 g) almond meal

1⅓ cups (7¾ oz/220 g) sugar

1 teaspoon ras el hanout*

1 teaspoon baking powder

4 eggs

1 cup (250 ml) olive oil

zest of 1 lemon

zest of 1 orange

2½ tablespoons lemon juice

⅓ cup (80 ml) orange juice

6 medjool dates, pitted

1 cinnamon stick

8–10 cardamom pods

2 star anise

Preparation time: 20 minutes • Cooking time: 45 minutes • Serves: 8

ARGAN OIL CHOCOLATE MUD BROWNIE WITH ORANGE CINNAMON ICE CREAM

After every meal in Morocco I was presented with a plate of freshly cut oranges dusted with cinnamon. While a great flavor combination in its own right, when turned into an ice cream and paired with this brownie, it's a killer dish that will have chocolate lovers begging for more.

ARGAN OIL CHOCOLATE MUD BROWNIE

Preheat the oven to 315°F (160°C). Line a baking tray with parchment paper.

Put the white and milk chocolate wafers on the prepared tray and bake for 10–15 minutes until combined and caramelized. Remove from the oven and set aside to cool, then break up into smaller pieces.

Mix the eggs and sugar in an electric stand mixer with the whisk attachment for 5 minutes on moderate–high speed or until soft peaks form. Set aside.

Melt the dark chocolate with the butter then stir in the argan oil. Add the dark chocolate mixture to the eggs and sugar and mix well until combined. Add the sour cream, cocoa powder, baking powder, and salt and fold through with the broken up pieces of caramelized chocolate.

Grease an 8¼ x 4¼ inch (21 x 11 cm) loaf pan. Pour in the mixture and bake for 45 minutes or until a skewer comes out clean and the top is slightly cracked.

ORANGE AND CINNAMON ICE CREAM

Heat the orange juice, zest, and sugar in a saucepan over low heat, stirring to dissolve the sugar. Remove from the heat and set aside to cool.

Beat the egg yolks in a bowl with a whisk and add to the cooled orange mixture. Add the vanilla seeds, cinnamon, and orange extract.

Whip the cream to soft peaks using an electric stand mixer with a whisk attachment. Fold the orange mixture into the cream.

Pour the combined mixture into a container and freeze for 2–3 hours. Allow to soften slightly before serving.

TO SERVE

Cut the argan oil chocolate mud brownie into slices and serve with a scoop of orange and cinnamon ice cream.

Note You can also make this brownie in a traditional brownie pan. It will take less time to cook. Try adding nuts for a different flavor and texture.

Argan oil chocolate mud brownie

2½ oz (75 g) white chocolate melting wafers (or white chocolate chips)

2½ oz (75 g) milk chocolate melting wafers (or milk chocolate chips)

3 eggs

generous 1 cup (8 oz/230 g) light brown sugar

7 oz (200 g) dark chocolate

4½ tablespoons (2¼ oz/60 g) butter

¼ cup (60 ml) argan oil*

⅓ cup (2½ oz/75 g) sour cream

⅓ cup (1 oz/30 g) dark unsweetened cocoa powder

1 teaspoon baking powder

pinch of salt

Orange and cinnamon ice cream

1 cup (250 ml) orange juice

grated zest of 2 oranges

⅔ cup (4½ oz/125 g) sugar

8 egg yolks

1 vanilla bean, split and seeds scraped

2 teaspoons ground cinnamon

2 teaspoons orange extract

4 cups (1 liter) whipping cream

Vejer de la Frontera

ANDALUSIA
SPAIN

I have often wondered during my travels around the Middle East how it was possible for the once awe-inspiring art, medicine, education, and architecture in this region to be so far ahead of the West and then suddenly just stop and, if anything, go backwards.

On my Moorish travels, journeying from Morocco to Andalusia, a part of modern Spain, this question was once again rolling around in my mind. Don't get me wrong, I loved Morocco. The hustle and bustle, excitement and energy in the street, beautiful people and landscapes, but to see where Morocco is today and what became of Andalusia since the Moors were kicked out almost 600 years ago, is nothing less than astonishing.

In every country I have traveled to, I have been repeatedly stopped in my tracks by reminders of a past glory and opulence. Breathtaking mosques and palaces in Iran and Turkey, the world's first universities in North Africa. I heard people talk about the wisdom and science that emerged from the Middle Eastern Islamic world—poets, artists, and a refined and civilized way of life surrounded by beauty, tranquility, and balance—forward-thinking people who were the leaders and pioneers of their day.

It seems the best of what was brought by the Moors, who ruled this part of Spain for almost 800 years, had been picked up and taken to a new level when it crossed the Straits of Gibraltar. This pocket at the bottom of Spain embraced all the beauty and splendor of Moorish culture and ran with it—expanding on the Moorish ideals and achieving harmony and balance. I am in love with Andalusia in every way. There is a real sense of community, family, and tradition, paired with a relaxed way of life that really appeals to me.

As soon as I touched down in Jerez I felt relaxed. The air was bright, the light dazzling, and there was a hum in the streets that didn't come from traffic or the commotion of people rushing around as it does back at home—it was a gentle, soothing hum of happiness that seemed to be bouncing all around the town.

My first meal—the first tapas bar I stepped into that night—was amazing. Real food cooked by real people and eaten by diners going about their everyday business. It wasn't a special night out, it was just dinner time. There was nobody instagramming their dishes, no one critiquing their meal on TripAdvisor, or looking over their shoulder to see who was looking at them or who was at the next table. It was just people getting together and enjoying life—people just happy to be there.

BAY OF BISCAY

SPAIN

PORTUGAL

✕ Cordoba

Seville ♣ ANDALUSIA

Jerez ✖ Malaga ✖ Granada

✱ Vejer de la Frontera

Straits of Gibraltar

MOROCCO

N

Later, I walked down a street and found myself irresistibly drawn into a peña (folk club) by the wail of singing and guitars, and the lustful rhythm of flamenco, belting out stories of new and lost love. WOW, I thought, is this really what life can be?

Next stop, Vejer de la Frontera. Let me just say, through my whole journey, I have been looking for a place I could call home, and this town could well be it. Situated about an hour's drive from the closest airport, 30 minutes to the beach, and about a two-hour drive to Seville, this 1400-year-old fortified town looks, for all its worth, like a whole ton of sugar cubes has been scattered over the top of a hill. From it, you can see the rolling green fields of the Cadiz countryside and on the horizon the glittering Straits of Gibraltar and the coastline of Morocco. And along its winding roads and impossibly narrow lanes, tiny hidden tapas bars, markets, and fabulous food shops run by the producers themselves.

I continued on my Andalusian odyssey—up and down the coast and all through the middle, visiting some beautiful cities and witnessing a food scene that is alive and pumping. Chefs at every level living for what they do and passionately sharing their craft with anyone who wants to experience it. There's everything from local working-class tapas bars that produce the best pork-stuffed rolls you have ever tasted, to a place that the king of modern Spanish cuisine, Ferran Adrià, and the actual king of Spain go to munch on crunchy shrimp tortillitas. Even at the top of the tree, where new world chefs cook with Spanish flair and bravado, they seem to share a brotherhood and respect for each other's skill and the dishes they create.

Comrades rather than competitors, this mindset is evident among local farmers who have such a strong connection with their land and crops, and the fishermen of Barbate who fish the same sea my Phoenician ancestors did, using the same ancient fishing techniques. It's also evident among the jamón producers in the Sierra de Aracena whose dehesa (oak forest) provides the perfect living environment for Iberian pigs that become heavenly jamón iberico de bellota.

This is what is exciting about Andalusia. What they have is perfect just as it is, but instead of being complacent and leaving things the way they are, they look for new and inspiring ways to make the most of things. Not for money or glory, but because they can, because they should, and because their souls yearn for more for tomorrow than they have today. ✖

Let me just say, through my whole journey, I have been looking for a place I could call home, and this town could well be it.

TUNA TARTARE, HARISSA AIOLI WITH SPICED WAFER

Tuna is a big deal all over the world and it is no different in Spain. Especially in the Straits of Gibraltar where tuna fishing has been an art since the time of the Phoenicians. These guys take their tuna fishing and cooking very seriously, and no part of the fish is wasted. In my opinion, tuna is best eaten raw, simply dressed, letting the natural texture and flavor of the fish do all the talking.

This dish pays homage to the flavors of Andalusia and the great tuna fishermen along the southern shore. The mojama brings a salty, strong fishy flavor into play, which works really well with the fresh tuna tartare.

Mix all the harissa aioli ingredients together in a bowl.

Put the tuna in a bowl and add a few spoonfuls of the harissa aioli to loosely bind. Add the remaining ingredients and mix together. Place in the fridge to chill.

Preheat the oven to 350°F (180°C).

Brush the pastry with the olive oil and place on a baking tray. Finely grate the almonds over the top and scatter over the remaining ingredients, except the mojama. Bake for 15 minutes or until golden.

Place a spoonful of the tuna on each plate. Dollop with some harissa aioli. Surround with shards of brik pastry and grate over the mojama.

Notes This is a great dish for when you're entertaining, since it's quick and easy to make the tuna.

Mojama is a salt-cured tuna. You only need a small amount as it packs a big flavor. It is available at specialty food stores. It can also be purchased online.

Harissa aioli
1 cup (8½ oz/235 g) aioli
   (or mayonnaise)
1 tablespoon harissa*
1 teaspoon smoked paprika

Tuna tartare
14 oz (400 g) sashimi-grade tuna,
   diced
½ cup (3¼ oz/90 g) green Spanish
   olives, pitted and diced
2 French shallots, diced
2½ tablespoons chopped chives
pinch of sea salt
⅓ cup (80 ml) olive oil

Spiced wafer
4 sheets brik pastry*
olive oil, for brushing
¼ cup (1 oz/30 g) blanched almonds
heaped 1 tablespoon thyme leaves
heaped 1 tablespoon coriander
   seeds, crushed
zest of 2 lemons
¾ oz (20 g) mojama (see note)

MOORISH CHILLED ALMOND AND ORANGE BLOSSOM SOUP WITH APPLE AND WATERCRESS DRESSING

This is a great soup, awesome on a hot summer's day. I couldn't believe how easy it was and for a dish with such ancient origins, how beautiful and complex the flavor profile could be.

Put the almonds, garlic, bread, and apple in a food processor and whiz until a paste is formed. With the machine running, slowly add a generous ¾ cup (200 ml) of water, then add the olive oil and 1½ tablespoons of the sherry vinegar. Next, add the orange blossom water, adjusting to taste if necessary. Season with salt, then pour into a jug and refrigerate for 2 hours to chill.

Finely chop the shrimp and mix in a bowl with the chili, cilantro, lemon zest, salt to taste, and the remaining vinegar. Drizzle with olive oil. Cover and refrigerate for 30 minutes to cure.

Make the dressing by mixing together the apple, almonds, chives, and watercress with enough olive oil to coat and salt to season.

Place the chilled soup in individual bowls, add the shrimp, and finish with the apple and watercress dressing and a drizzle of olive oil.

Note You can grill or sauté the shrimp if you prefer them cooked.

¾ cup (3½ oz/100 g) blanched almonds
1 garlic clove
2 thick slices day-old bread, soaked in water until soft
½ green apple, peeled, quartered, and chopped
scant ½ cup (100 ml) extra virgin olive oil, plus 1 tablespoon extra
⅓ cup (80 ml) sherry vinegar
1 teaspoon orange blossom water*
pinch of sea salt
8 large raw shrimp (shrimp), peeled and deveined, tails removed (see note)
1 small red chili, seeds removed, diced
1 tablespoon finely chopped cilantro
zest of 1 lemon

Apple and watercress dressing
1 green apple, peeled, cored, and finely diced
handful sliced almonds
heaped 1 tablespoon chopped chives
handful watercress, leaves picked
drizzle of extra virgin olive oil
pinch of sea salt

SALMOREJO PURÉE WITH JAMON, QUAIL EGG, GREEN APPLE, AND SHERRY DRESSING

I was a bit sceptical about this dish before I ate it. I thought what is all the fuss about? It's just a thick gazpacho, how good could it be? Well, let me tell you it is the bomb!

Instead of making the salmorejo the star of the show I have turned it into a refresher of sorts and turned up the flavors that accompany this great dish.

I hope I have done it some justice.

PICKLED QUAIL EGGS

Combine all the ingredients except the eggs in a small saucepan over medium heat. Bring to a boil, then simmer for 3 minutes. Remove from the heat and leave to cool.

Place the eggs in a sterilized jar and pour over the vinegar mixture. Refrigerate for 24 hours before using.

SALMOREJO PURÉE

Place all the ingredients in a food processor and blend until thick and smooth. Check and adjust the seasoning to taste.

ALMOND PURÉE

Put the almonds and milk in a saucepan over medium heat and cook for 20 minutes or until the almonds are soft. Remove from the heat and blend in a food processor until silky smooth. Blend in the olive oil and sherry vinegar to taste.

SPICY PORK

Heat the olive oil and jamon fat in a frying pan over medium heat. Add the pork, bay leaf, paprika, onion, and garlic, and cook until the pork is crispy. Remove and set aside.

Pickled quail eggs

½ cup (120 ml) white wine vinegar

¼ cup (60 ml) dry white wine

1 teaspoon fennel seeds

1 teaspoon coriander seeds

1 teaspoon black peppercorns

½ teaspoon smoked paprika

½ teaspoon sea salt

2 French shallots, sliced

1 bay leaf

6 boiled quail eggs, peeled (see note)

Salmorejo purée

4 tomatoes, chopped

1 green pepper, chopped

2 garlic cloves

2 slices bread, soaked in a little water

¼ cup (60 ml) olive oil

dash of Tabasco

pinch of saffron threads

2 tablespoons sherry vinegar

Almond purée

1 cup (5½ oz/150 g) blanched almonds

3⅓ cups (800 ml) milk

½ cup (120 ml) olive oil

2 tablespoons sherry vinegar

Spicy pork

2½ tablespoons olive oil

1½ oz (40 g) jamon fat

14 oz (400 g) ground pork

1 bay leaf

2 teaspoons smoked paprika

1 yellow onion, diced

1 garlic clove, diced

Sherry dressing

½ cup (120 ml) Spanish sherry
2 French shallots, finely diced
1 teaspoon coriander seeds
2½ tablespoons chopped toasted
    almonds
2½ tablespoons chopped chives
1 tablespoon sherry vinegar
splash of olive oil

To serve

8 thin jamon slices, torn
2 green apples, scooped into balls
handful baby radishes, thinly sliced
1 turnip, peeled and very thinly sliced
6 chives, cut into 1¼ inch (3 cm)
    lengths
handful frisee leaves

SHERRY DRESSING

Put the sherry in a small saucepan over high heat. Bring to a boil and cook until the sherry has reduced by half. Add the shallots, coriander seeds, almonds, chives, and sherry vinegar. Set aside to cool. When cool, add enough olive oil to make a dressing. Check and adjust the seasoning.

TO SERVE

Place some almond purée around the base of each plate. Scatter over the crispy pork. Cut the quail eggs in half and place two halves on each plate. Scatter the jamon, apple, radish, turnip, chives, and frisee around the rim of the plate and dress with some of the sherry dressing.

Serve with small bowls of salmorejo.

Notes To ensure the yolks are centerd in the eggs, stir them while in the boiling water. For a hard-boiled white with a soft runny yolk, put the eggs into a small saucepan of boiling water and cook for 2½ minutes. Remove and cool in iced water. Removing the shell is easier if the egg is cold.

Salmorejo purée with
jamon, quail egg,
green apple, and sherry
dressing

Preparation time: 10 minutes • Cooking time: 20 minutes • Serves: 8

POACHED LOBSTER PRINGA WITH GAZPACHO-FLAVORED MAYONNAISE AND CRISPY SHRIMP

There is no way in the world I could even begin to try to cook a pork pringa like the one I had in Seville. It was the best sandwich I have ever eaten, hands down.

I think what really caught me by surprise was the unsteadiness of this pringa. It just looked like a dry overcooked little bread roll with not much going on. Boy, was I wrong! Jammed into the middle of a crunchy moist little roll was fatty, salty meaty goodness that almost knocked me off my seat.

Anyway, this is my take. Like I said, I didn't want to try to imitate it, so I just drew on some of the textures and tried to bring out some of the flavors. I hope you like it!

1 lobster tail (about 14 oz–1 lb 2 oz/ 400–500 g)

1 lb 2 oz (500 g) raw shrimp, peeled and roughly chopped

2½ tablespoons all-purpose flour

canola oil, for deep-frying

2½ tablespoons smoked paprika, for dusting

8 small bread rolls, halved

olive oil, for frying

handful watercress, leaves picked

Gazpacho-flavored mayonnaise

1 cup (8½ oz/235 g) mayonnaise

2½ tablespoons ketchup

1 teaspoon Tabasco sauce

½ Lebanese or Persian cucumber, peeled and finely diced

½ red onion, finely diced

6 Italian parsley stems, leaves picked and chopped

6 mint stems, leaves picked and chopped

To cook the lobster tail, place it in a small saucepan and cover with lightly salted water. Bring to a boil, reduce the heat to a simmer, and cook for 8–12 minutes until the shell turns bright red and the meat is tender. For larger or smaller tails, adjust the cooking time as needed. Remove from the heat and drain.

Meanwhile, to make the gazpacho-flavored mayonnaise, mix all the ingredients together in a bowl. Season with salt and freshly ground black pepper and set aside.

Remove the shrimp meat from the shells, place in a bowl, and coat lightly in the flour.

Pour some canola oil into a deep frying pan to a depth of about 1½ inches (4 cm), then heat over medium–high heat until it shimmers. If you have a kitchen thermometer, the oil will be ready when the temperature reaches 350°F (180°C). Alternatively, use a deep-fryer.

Carefully add the shrimp to the pan and deep-fry for a few minutes until crisp and crunchy. Remove and drain on paper towels. Toss with some paprika to season.

Heat a frying pan over high heat. Drizzle the bread rolls with olive oil, season with salt and pepper, and fry until crisp and crunchy on the outside.

Gently tear the lobster into bite-sized pieces. Place in a bowl and toss with some of the gazpacho-flavored mayonnaise and the watercress.

Fill the fried bread rolls with the lobster and mayo mixture, top with the shrimp, and serve immediately.

Note For a change, serve with small bowls of traditional gazpacho.

OLIVE OIL POACHED POTATOES, PICKLED OCTOPUS, AND GREEN OLIVES

This is a typical Spanish tapas that you will find all throughout Andalusia, although every tapas bar will have their own subtle little twist on it that makes it theirs.

This is my little twist—I think the introduction of octopus and some bitter orange zest gives it a slight edge over some of the ones I tried in Spain.

Place all the pickled octopus ingredients in a large non-metallic bowl with 2 cups (500 ml) of water. Cover with plastic wrap and place in the fridge for 12 hours. Remove and drain. Discard the liquid.

Place the potatoes in a saucepan and cover with cold water. Add a pinch of salt, bring to a boil over medium–high heat, and cook for 15 minutes or until tender when tested with a sharp knife. Remove from the heat, drain, and break each in half. Toss the potatoes in the olive oil and allow them to absorb the oil. Drizzle with the vinegar, season with salt and pepper, and set aside.

Heat a grill pan over high heat. When hot, grill the octopus for a couple of minutes until charred and just cooked through. Season with salt and pepper. Remove and slice into bite-sized pieces.

Toss the octopus with the potatoes, and add the olives, shallot, scallions, garlic, and parsley. Top with the seville orange zest and smoked paprika, and serve.

Note Kiwi contains a natural enzyme that helps to tenderize the octopus.

Pickled octopus

2 lb 4 oz (1 kg) baby octopus, cleaned, beaks removed
3 tablespoons white vinegar
1 kiwi, peeled and puréed (see note)
2 teaspoons salt
1 garlic clove, sliced
1 bay leaf
5 thyme sprigs
1 teaspoon smoked paprika

1 lb 12 oz (800 g) mixed potatoes
1 cup (250 ml) Spanish olive oil
2½ tablespoons sherry vinegar
1 cup (6 oz/175 g) green Spanish olives, pitted and roughly chopped
1 French shallot, diced
4 scallions, thinly sliced
1 large garlic clove
2½ tablespoons chopped Italian parsley
zest of 1 seville orange
2 teaspoons smoked paprika

BRAISED PIG'S EARS, MORCILLA, QUAIL EGGS, AND JAMON

Tapas bars in Spain all have their own soul and personality. They have dishes they do well and then they have dishes that they do darn well. The food in general in Andalusia is humblingly good. This dish is my homage to the flavors and products of good Spanish tapas.

BRAISED PIG'S EARS

Bring a saucepan of water to a boil. Place the pig's ears in the water and parboil for a few minutes to remove any scum and impurities.

Remove the ears from the water and place in a clean saucepan. Add enough water to cover both ears. Add the onion, carrot, and herbs. Bring to a boil over medium–high heat, then reduce the heat and simmer for 2½ hours or until the ears are very soft. Remove from the pan and slice into strips.

CARAMELIZED ONION DRESSING

Cook the onions and olive oil in a wide heavy-based frying pan over low heat for about 30 minutes until golden and caramelized. Remove from the heat and allow to cool. Once cool, strain over a bowl, reserving the oil, then finely chop the onions.

Put the chopped onions back into the oil and add the sherry vinegar and mustard to taste.

ALMOND PURÉE

Put the almonds and milk in a saucepan over medium heat and cook for 20 minutes or until the almonds are soft. Remove from the heat and blend in a food processor until silky smooth. Blend in the olive oil and sherry vinegar to taste.

Braised pig's ears

2 pigs ears (about 2¾–3½ oz/ 80–100 g each)
1 onion, cut into large pieces
1 carrot, peeled and quartered
a few sprigs each of thyme, oregano, and bay leaves

Caramelized onion dressing

2 yellow onions, thinly sliced
1 cup (250 ml) olive oil
¼ cup (60 ml) sherry vinegar, or to taste
1 teaspoon wholegrain mustard, or to taste

Almond purée

½ cup (2¾ oz/80 g) blanched almonds
1¾ cups (400 ml) milk
¼ cup (60 ml) olive oil, or to taste
2 tablespoons sherry vinegar, or to taste

To assemble

canola oil, for deep-frying
all-purpose flour, for dusting
2½ tablespoons olive oil
1 morcilla sausage, sliced
1 slice day-old bread, torn into pieces
heaped 1 tablespoon smoked paprika
heaped 1 tablespoon sherry vinegar
handful Italian parsley, leaves picked and torn
2 tablespoons (1 oz/30 g) butter
4 quail eggs
8 thin slices jamon
2–3 cups (3½ oz/100 g) mixed salad greens and watercress, to serve
extra virgin olive oil, to serve

TO ASSEMBLE

Pour some canola oil into a deep frying pan to a depth of about 1½ inches (4 cm), then heat over medium–high heat until it shimmers. If you have a kitchen thermometer, the oil will be ready when the temperature reaches 350°F (180°C). Alternatively, use a deep-fryer.

Dust the braised pig's ears in flour and deep fry for a few minutes until crispy and crunchy. Remove and drain on paper towels and sprinkle with salt and pepper to season.

Heat the olive oil in a medium frying pan over medium heat and fry the morcilla sausage until golden brown. Add the bread and cook in the sausage pan juices until golden and crunchy. Add 2 tablespoons of the onion dressing to the pan. Sprinkle with the paprika. Finish with the sherry vinegar and torn parsley.

In a separate frying pan, melt the butter over low heat and then gently fry the quail eggs until just cooked. Season with salt and pepper and set aside.

To serve, brush some almond purée across each plate. Layer some slices of jamon, and top with the pig's ears, morcilla sausage, and croutons. Add the salad greens, drizzle with some extra virgin olive oil, and top with a fried quail egg.

Notes The caramelized onion dressing can be kept in the fridge for up to 1 week. The olive oil will become solid from refrigerating, so allow it to come to room temperature before using.

When braising the pig's ears, you can double the quantity and freeze the extra for next time.

You can use a pressure cooker to halve the cooking time for the pig's ears.

Braised pig's ears,
morcilla, quail eggs,
and jamon

RABO DE KANGAROO WITH ROAST JERUSALEM ARTICHOKES

It's funny how this dish came about; I had just eaten the best rabo de toro in all of Andalusia and I was licking the plate it was so good. Then I got talking to the restaurant owner and he said they use the tails from bullfight bulls to make the dish. Now, irrespective of your political stance on bullfighting, this is an amazing dish and we started joking about how if we were to do it in Australia, maybe we could use a "fighting kangaroo?" And then bang, this dish was born. (Kangaroo tail isn't available in many parts of the world but other red meats will do well in this recipe, see note.)

Combine the paprika, saffron powder, and nutmeg. Rub the mixture over the kangaroo (or other meat) to coat well.

Put the meat in a heavy-based saucepan or Dutch oven and place over high heat. Cook for a few minutes, turning occasionally to brown all over and seal the sides. Remove from the pan and set aside.

Heat the olive oil in the pan, then add the onions, pancetta, garlic, bay leaves, peppercorns, cinnamon sticks, and cloves. Cook for 10 minutes, stirring occasionally until the onion is very soft. Deglaze with the sherry and reduce the liquid by half. Return the meat to the pan, along with the tomato, and cover with about 2 cups (500 ml) of water. Cover with a lid and cook for 1½ hours or until the meat is falling apart.

Meanwhile, put the artichokes, lemon juice, thyme, peppercorns, garlic, bay leaf, and 4 cups (1 liter) of water in a saucepan and bring to a boil over medium–high heat. Reduce the heat to low and simmer for 20 minutes or until the artichokes are soft when pierced with a sharp knife. Drain, then transfer to a tray lined with paper towels. Put in the fridge for 30 minutes to dry completely.

Preheat the oven to 400°F (200°C). Drizzle the oil into a roasting pan and place in the oven to heat.

Place the artichokes in the hot roasting pan and carefully toss in the oil. Cook for 30 minutes until golden and crunchy, turning as required.

Remove the artichokes from the oven and place in a large frying pan with a little extra oil over high heat. Add the Aleppo pepper, smoked paprika, parsley, and lemon zest, and toss to combine the flavors for a few minutes. Season with salt and the sherry vinegar.

To serve, plate up the meat and serve with the roasted artichokes.

Note Any other red meat cuts suitable for braising would be a good substitute in this dish.

Rabo de kangaroo

2 teaspoons smoked paprika

pinch saffron powder

1 nutmeg, finely grated

2 lb 4 oz (1 kg) kangaroo tail pieces (or other braising cuts of meat, see note)

2½ tablespoons olive oil

1 lb 2 oz (500 g) onions, chopped

14 oz (400 g) flat pancetta, skin removed, chopped

1 garlic bulb, halved crossways

3 bay leaves

1 teaspoon black peppercorns, crushed

3 cinnamon sticks

10 cloves

scant 2 cups (450 ml) Oloroso sherry

1 lb 5 oz (600 g) tomatoes, grated

Roast Jerusalem artichokes

2 lb 4 oz (1 kg) Jerusalem artichokes (sunchokes), scrubbed and halved

2½ tablespoons lemon juice

a few thyme sprigs

heaped 1 tablespoon black peppercorns

2 garlic cloves

1 bay leaf

⅓ cup (80 ml) olive oil, plus extra for frying

1 teaspoon Aleppo pepper*

1 teaspoon smoked paprika

2 handfuls Italian parsley, leaves picked

zest of 1 lemon

2½ tablespoons sherry vinegar

BRAISED RABBIT WITH ARTICHOKE AND PEA SALAD

My new food hero Charo Carmona of Arte de Cozina in Antequera has touched my heart in a way no other cook has. She is a real foodie who has dedicated her life to the preservation of the food culture of her region. She not only cooks the food of her homeland, but works with producers to ensure the products she needs are still grown in their natural habitats so future generations can enjoy the cuisine of this great food region.

Her passion for the food she cooked for me made every mouthful taste even better and, to be honest, I never wanted to leave her kitchen. This is one of the dishes she shared with me.

I hope I can make it back to Antequera one day and spend a whole day eating and drinking in Charo's restaurant.

Set aside the belly flaps, liver, and kidneys. Cut the rabbit into 8 pieces.

Put the olive oil and sliced garlic in a heavy-based saucepan over low heat and gently cook. When the garlic starts to turn golden, remove from the oil and set aside.

Increase the heat to medium, add the rabbit liver and kidneys, and chicken livers to the pan and cook for 2–3 minutes until browned. Remove and set aside.

Reduce the heat to low, add the rabbit pieces, and cook for 10 minutes, turning occasionally until evenly browned. Season with salt and freshly ground white pepper. Add the paprika and stir well. Add the onions, cinnamon sticks, bay leaf, and saffron powder. Increase the heat to high and deglaze the pan with the sherry vinegar. Cook for a few minutes to reduce. Cover with about 4 cups (1 liter) of boiling water and simmer for 45 minutes or until the meat falls off the bone.

Meanwhile, cook the artichoke hearts in a saucepan of lightly salted boiling water over medium–high heat for 20 minutes or until tender. (You can also boil or steam the leaves for another use.) Remove from the pan and set aside.

Use a mallet to flatten the rabbit belly flaps, slice thinly, and season with salt and freshly ground black pepper. Rest for 10 minutes.

Wash the salt off the rabbit flaps, pat dry with paper towels, and dust lightly with flour.

Pour some canola oil into a frying pan to a depth of about 1½ inches (4 cm), then heat over medium–high heat until it shimmers. If you have a kitchen

Braised rabbit

1 large farmed rabbit (about 4 lb 8 oz/2 kg), belly flaps, liver, and kidneys reserved

2 cups (500 ml) olive oil

1 garlic bulb, peeled and thinly sliced

7 oz (200 g) chicken livers

2½ tablespoons smoked paprika

2 yellow onions, sliced

2 cinnamon sticks

1 bay leaf

1 teaspoon saffron powder

1 cup (250 ml) sherry vinegar

1 loaf day-old bread, cut into large chunks

Artichoke and pea salad

4 artichoke hearts

reserved rabbit belly flaps (see above)

2½ tablespoons all-purpose flour

canola oil, for deep-frying

⅔ cup (3½ oz/100 g) toasted almonds, roughly chopped

scant ½ cup (100 ml) olive oil

heaped 1 tablespoon lemon juice

1 small frisee, leaves picked

9 oz (250 g) fresh peas

2 lb 4 oz (1 kg) fresh fava beans, podded and peeled

6 slices jamon

thermometer, the oil will be ready when the temperature reaches 350°F (180°C). Alternatively, use a deep-fryer.

Carefully put the rabbit flaps in the oil and deep-fry for a few minutes until crunchy. Remove and drain on paper towels.

Carefully add the bread to the same pan and deep-fry for a few minutes until golden. Transfer onto paper towels to drain.

Meanwhile, remove the rabbit pieces from the saucepan, leave to cool slightly, then pick the meat from the bones. Set aside the meat and discard the bones. Reserve the cooking liquid.

Add the fried bread to the reserved cooking liquid with the cooked garlic, kidneys, and livers. Transfer into a food processor and purée until thick and creamy. Adjust the seasoning. Return to the pan, fold in the picked meat, and cover with a lid.

Combine the almonds, olive oil, and lemon juice in a small bowl to make a dressing. Place the frisee in a salad bowl with the artichoke, peas, fava beans, and rabbit belly. Scatter with the jamon and toss in the dressing.

Divide the braised rabbit between eight serving plates and serve with the artichoke and pea salad.

Note This recipe only uses the artichoke hearts, but you can keep the leaves for another use. To obtain the hearts, trim off the leaves, and scoop out and discard the hairy "choke." You can stop the artichokes from discoloring by placing it in a bowl of water with a lemon half.

Braised rabbit
with artichoke
and pea salad

Preparation time: 20 minutes • Cooking time: 50 minutes • Serves: 4

SQUID INK RICE WITH CHORIZO-FILLED BABY CALAMARI AND SEAWEED

I remember cooking squid ink risotto as a commis chef and falling in love with it back then, so to see it in Spain was like falling in love all over again. The introduction of the nori was a great little touch, which I loved, and chorizo is a winner with any type of seafood in my book.

I have used cuttlefish, a marine cephalopod common in Spanish cooking, but you can easily substitute more widely available squid in this recipe.

Heat 2 tablespoons of the olive oil in a frying pan over medium–high heat. Add the chorizo and cook for a few minutes, turning often until well colored and crisp. Add the cuttlefish or squid, parsley, and chili and toss to combine. Continue to cook until the cuttlefish or squid is opaque and just cooked. Remove the chorizo mixture from the pan, transfer to a bowl, and leave to cool.

Place ½ cup (3¾ oz/110 g) of the rice in a small saucepan with enough water to cover by ½ inch (1 cm). Bring to a boil, cover with a lid, and cook for 10 minutes or until the water is absorbed and the rice is plump. Remove from the heat and place in a bowl to cool.

Add the breadcrumbs, cooked rice, and egg to the chorizo mixture, season with salt and pepper, and mix well. Stuff the baby calamari with the mixture and secure the ends with toothpicks. Set aside.

Heat the remaining oil in a large deep-sided frying pan over high heat. Add the onions and garlic and cook until soft. Add the remaining 1 cup (7¾ oz/220 g) of rice to the pan and cook for a few minutes until the rice is slightly translucent. Deglaze the pan with the sherry and wine and stir well. Add the squid ink and fish stock, reduce the heat to low, and cook for 15 minutes or until the rice is almost cooked. Season with nutmeg, fold in the butter, nestle the stuffed calamari in the rice, and continue to cook for another few minutes until the calamari is just cooked and the rice is tender. Remove the toothpicks and divide the calamari between four shallow bowls, spoon over the rice, sprinkle on the nori shards, if using, and serve.

Note You can make this dish without the squid ink, if it is unavailable at your fishmonger's.

scant ½ cup (100 ml) olive oil

2 large chorizo sausages, skin removed and meat finely diced

2 cuttlefish or squid (about 7 oz/200 g each), cleaned and finely chopped

2½ tablespoons chopped Italian parsley

1 long red chili, seeded and finely chopped

1½ cups (11½ oz/330 g) arborio rice (or vialone rice)

½ cup (1 oz/30 g) fresh breadcrumbs

1 egg, beaten

8 baby calamari (about 2¾ oz/80 g each), cleaned

4 yellow onions, finely diced

2 garlic cloves, sliced

scant ½ cup (100 ml) sherry (preferably Pedro Ximénez)

1 cup (250 ml) sweet white wine

2 teaspoons squid ink (see note)

2 cups (500 ml) fish stock

pinch of freshly grated nutmeg

2 tablespoons (1 oz/30 g) butter

2 sheets nori, fried, broken into shards (optional)

TORTILLAS DE CAMARONES AND PORK BELLY ON BRIOCHE BUNS

The ability to make good tortillas de camarones is one of the trademarks of a good cook in Spain—crunchy shellfish fritters that crumble in your mouth with every bite. They are very tasty, but can be very oily and messy. When I was eating them I kept thinking they would be great in a sandwich like pork rind in a roast pork roll. And now that I have it, I hope you enjoy it, too.

Heat the olive oil in a heavy-based saucepan or Dutch oven over medium–high heat. Add the onions, garlic, and carrots and cook for a few minutes to soften. Add the pork, sherry, and enough water to cover. Bring to a boil, then reduce the heat, cover with a lid, and cook for 2 hours until the pork is falling apart.

Meanwhile, to make the tortillas de camarones, mix the flour and eggs in a bowl. Add a scant ½ cup (100 ml) of water and stir to make a smooth batter. Add the scallions, onion, parsley, dried shrimp. and fresh shrimp. Season with salt, pepper, and the paprika. Cover in plastic wrap and refrigerate for 30 minutes.

Heat 2 tablespoons of olive oil in a frying pan over high heat. Spoon in 2 tablespoons of the batter, flatten with the back of a wooden spoon, and cook for about 3 minutes until golden. Flip and cook the other side for the same length of time. Repeat with the remaining mixture to make 8 fritters. Drain on paper towels.

Remove the saucepan from the heat and transfer the pork to a warm platter. Leave to cook slightly and then roughly shred.

In a bowl, mix the aioli with the roasted garlic and lemon zest and juice. Fold in the red onion and parsley. Add the sherry vinegar.

Spread some garlic aioli on the base of each bun. Add some shredded pork, then a tortilla de camarones fritter, top with the bun lid, and serve immediately.

Note Dried shrimp are available from Asian supermarkets.
Look for the smallest school shrimp you can find. Leave them unpeeled, for extra crunch—so the smaller the better.

2½ tablespoons olive oil
2 yellow onions, thinly sliced
4 garlic cloves
2 carrots, peeled and sliced
2 lb 4 oz (1 kg) pork belly
2 cups (500 ml) Oloroso sherry
1 cup (8½ oz/235 g) aioli
　(or mayonnaise)
2 garlic cloves, roasted and smashed
zest and juice of 1 lemon
1 red onion, thinly sliced
handful Italian parsley, leaves picked
2 teaspoons sherry vinegar
8 small brioche or soft buns, halved
　and toasted

Tortillas de camarones
generous ½ cup (2½ oz/75 g)
　all-purpose flour
2 eggs
4 scallions, finely chopped
1 yellow onion, finely diced
2½ tablespoons chopped Italian
　parsley
2½ tablespoons dried shrimp
　(see note)
9 oz (250 g) small school shrimp
　(see note)
pinch of smoked paprika
olive oil, for shallow-frying

Cádiz

SALT-CRUSTED FRUITS OF THE SEA WITH JAMON AND SHERRY CREAM

Baking fish in salt is one of the most beautiful ways to enhance the natural sea-salt flavors naturally found in fish. It is a technique that is as old as the hills and, done right, it can be the show-stopper of the night. I loved the theater of breaking of the crust and wanted to do this at my restaurant, Maha. So I introduced a little sweet sherry and fennel to the original dish to help finesse the flavors. I know this is a little old school, but, hey, sometimes old school is the only school!

Preheat the oven to 400°F (200°C).

Put the olive oil and butter in a large saucepan over medium heat to melt. Thinly slice one of the fennel bulbs and add to the pan with the onions and garlic. Cook for about 5 minutes until softened. Add the bay leaves and thyme and season with salt and white pepper. Add the sherry and deglaze the pan, then bring to a gentle simmer for 2–3 minutes, stirring well until reduced. Add the cream and continue to cook for 6–8 minutes until thickened and reduced further. Check the seasoning. Remove from the heat and strain through a sieve into a bowl.

Divide the seafood between four 1½ cup (375 ml) ovenproof ramekins. Add the potatoes, the remaining fennel bulbs, and the eel, jamon, and parsley. Top with the sauce and season with plenty of salt and pepper. (See note.)

Divide the pastry sheet into four. Cut the pastry squares into rounds and place on top of the ramekins. Brush with the beaten egg, season with salt, sprinkle with the paprika, then place in the oven and cook for 20 minutes or until the pastry is golden and crisp.

Remove from the oven and serve.

Note You don't need to fill the ramekins to the top. The gap between the pastry lid and the seafood allows it to cook quickly.

2½ tablespoons olive oil

2½ tablespoons (1¼ oz/35 g) butter

5 small fennel bulbs

2 red onions, thinly sliced

2 garlic cloves, sliced

2 bay leaves

a few thyme sprigs

pinch of white pepper

1 cup (250 ml) dry sherry
   (such as Manzanilla or Fino)

2 cups (500 ml) whipping cream

2 lb 4 oz (1 kg) mixed fresh seafood
   (including clams, mussels, oysters,
   scallops, and white fish pieces)

4 small potatoes, peeled and boiled
   or roasted

½ smoked eel (about 7 oz/200 g),
   skin and bones removed

3½ oz (100 g) shaved jamon

¼ cup (½ oz/15 g) chopped Italian
   parsley

1 sheet puff pasty, thawed

1 egg yolk, beaten

pinch of smoked paprika

Preparation time: 10 minutes • Cooking time: 3 hours • Serves: 6–8

BARBECUED PORK RIBS WITH FRIED EGGPLANT AND MOLASSES, AND SMOKED EGGPLANT DIP

Slow-cooking in a bitter, sweet, sticky glaze has to be one of the best ways to cook pork ribs, I think. I really enjoyed the way tapas bars in Spain would shallow-fry eggplant and then drizzle it in sugar cane molasses to offset the fatty, oily flavor of the deep-fried eggplant and help cut through any oily flavors that might be left on your palate. It gave me the idea to glaze pork ribs in the same way to help cut and caramelize the pork fat, and the smoked eggplant dip rounds out the dish.

Preheat the oven to 300°F (150°C).

Mix the barbecue sauce and molasses together in a bowl then baste the pork ribs generously with half of the sauce.

Place the ribs on a baking tray and cover tightly with foil. Bake for 2½ hours or until tender.

Meanwhile, to make the eggplant dip, cook the whole eggplants over a gas flame or barbecue for about 15 minutes until blackened and charred on all sides, turning with tongs. Remove from the heat and set aside to cool slightly. Peel the eggplants and discard the blackened skins. Place the flesh in a food processor with the tahini, garlic, and lemon juice and blend until smooth. Drizzle in the olive oil and season with salt. Set aside.

Increase the oven temperature to 400°F (200°C), remove the foil from the ribs, baste again with some of the remaining molasses mixture, and cook for about 15 minutes, until the ribs are sticky, dark, and golden.

When the ribs are almost cooked, cut the Lebanese eggplants into large cubes and dust with the flour.

Pour some canola oil into a deep frying pan to a depth of about 1½ inches (4 cm), then heat over medium–high heat until it shimmers. If you have a kitchen thermometer, the oil will be ready when the temperature reaches 350°F (180°C). Alternatively, use a deep-fryer. Carefully add the eggplant pieces and deep-fry for a few minutes until golden. Remove and drain on paper towels.

Put the deep-fried eggplants in a bowl and add the shallots, almonds, sherry vinegar, olive oil, and remaining molasses mixture. Toss gently. Garnish with some parsley.

Remove the ribs from the oven and cut them either side of the bone. Scatter with the jamon slices and some parsley, and serve with the fried eggplant and molasses and the smoked eggplant dip.

1 cup (250 ml) barbecue sauce

2 cups (500 ml) sugar cane molasses, plus 2 teaspoons extra

2 lb 4 oz (1 kg) baby back pork ribs

2 Lebanese (long thin) eggplants

all-purpose flour, for dusting

canola oil, for deep-frying

2 French shallots, diced

2½ tablespoons chopped toasted almonds

splash of sherry vinegar

drizzle of olive oil

Italian parsley leaves, to serve

jamon slices, to serve

Smoked eggplant dip

2 eggplants

2½ tablespoons tahini*

1 garlic clove

2½ tablespoons lemon juice

¼ cup (60 ml) olive oil

pinch of sea salt

ORANGE BLOSSOM TOCINOS CIELO WITH PEAR SORBET, CLOVE POWDER, AND YUZU

When I ate this dessert I couldn't believe how many egg yolks it had in it. It was full on! Then all of that sugar to finish it off with. Wow, it's a miracle that anyone in Seville has any teeth!

I wanted to give it a go back at Maha, so I added a little orange blossom to remind me of all the orange trees that line the streets of Seville and I introduced a fresh pear sorbet to help cut the custard and add a little fresh fruit flavor.

PEAR SORBET

Put the pears with their syrup in a food processor and blend until smooth. Place the purée and egg whites in the bowl of an electric stand mixer, attach the whisk attachment, and whisk at moderate speed until the mixture doubles in size.

Place the sugar and scant ½ cup (100 ml) of water in a small saucepan set over low heat. Stir until the sugar has dissolved, then increase the heat, bring to a boil, and cook to soft ball stage—drop a small amount into a shallow bowl of cold water. If ready, it will form a soft ball. If you have a kitchen thermometer, the syrup will be ready when the temperature reaches about 240°F (115–118°C).

Decrease the speed to low and slowly pour the syrup into the pear and egg white mixture. Then whisk at high speed for 3 minutes or until cold. Transfer to a container and freeze overnight.

ORANGE BLOSSOM TOCINOS CIELO

Preheat the oven to 300°F (150°C).

Put ⅔ cup (5½ oz/150 g) of the sugar in a small saucepan over medium–low heat. Cook, stirring frequently, until it melts and becomes a light caramel. Pour into a 9½ x 8 inch (24 x 20 cm) ovenproof container and set aside.

In a clean saucepan, combine the remaining sugar, blossom water, and just under ½ cup (115 ml) of water. Bring to a boil and cook until thickened—if you have a kitchen thermometer it will be ready when the temperature reaches 220°F (104°C).

Put the egg yolks in the bowl of an electric stand mixer with the whisk attachment and whisk at moderate–high speed to combine. Whisk in the sugar syrup and continue to whisk until cooled and thick.

Pour the mixture over the caramel in the container. Place the container in a larger shallow baking dish and place in the oven. Carefully pour hot water into the bottom baking dish to come halfway up the sides of the smaller container.

Pear sorbet
14 oz (400 g) canned pears in syrup
3 egg whites
1 cup (7 oz/200 g) superfine sugar

Orange blossom tocinos cielo
2 cups (14 oz/400 g) sugar
2 tablespoons orange blossom water*
8 egg yolks

Paprika meringue
6 large egg whites
⅔ cup (5 oz/140 g) brown sugar
1¼ cups (9 oz/250 g) sugar
sweet paprika, for dusting

Clove cookie crumbs
1⅓ cups (4½ oz/125 g) sliced almonds
2⅓ cups (10½ oz/300 g) all-purpose flour
scant ½ cup (3¼ oz/90 g) sugar
2 teaspoons ground cloves
1 teaspoon ground cinnamon
2¼ sticks (9 oz/250 g) butter, chilled and cubed
1 teaspoon natural vanilla extract

Yuzu puree
1½ cups (350 ml) yuzu juice
2½ tablespoons instant clear jel starch (see note) (or use tapioca or corn starch)

Place in the oven and bake for 30–40 minutes, until the custard is just set.

Carefully remove from the oven and from the water bath and allow to cool to room temperature. Cover with plastic wrap and refrigerate for 2 hours.

PAPRIKA MERINGUE

Preheat the oven to 235°F (120°C). Line a baking tray with parchment paper.

Fill the bottom of a double boiler (or use a saucepan) with water and place over low heat to bring to a simmer. Place the egg whites and sugars in the top of the double boiler (or a heatproof bowl that fits over the saucepan, ensuring the bowl doesn't come into contact with the water). Heat for approximately 5 minutes, or until a kitchen thermometer reaches 105°F (40°C).

Remove the mixture from the heat and place in the bowl of an electric stand mixer. Attach the whisk attachment and whisk at high speed for around 8 minutes, until the mixture has cooled.

Place spoonfuls of the mixture on the prepared tray, or use a pastry bag, allowing room for the meringues to expand. Sprinkle on the paprika through a fine sieve. Place the tray in the oven and bake for 1¼ hours. When they are ready, the meringues will be dry underneath, but still soft in the center.

Remove from the oven and allow to cool.

CLOVE COOKIE CRUMBS

Put the almonds in a food processor and process until finely ground. Add the flour, sugar, cloves, and cinnamon, and process to combine. Add the butter and vanilla, and pulse to form a dough.

Divide the dough into four, then roll out each piece into 16 inch (40 cm) logs, wrap in plastic wrap, place on a tray, and refrigerate for 30 minutes (the logs can be frozen at this stage).

When ready to bake, preheat the oven to 275°F (140°C).

Slice off ½ inch (1 cm) rounds, place on a baking tray lined with parchment paper, and bake for 20 minutes or until lightly colored.

Remove from the oven and set aside to cool slightly.

To make the crumbs, crumble the shortbread or pulse in a food processor.

YUZU PURÉE

Put the yuzu juice in a bowl with the gel cream and combine using a hand-held immersion blender until smooth and thickened.

TO SERVE

Invert the orange blossom tocinos cielo on a flat dish and cut into squares. Serve with pear sorbet, some clove cookie crumbs, yuzu purée, and paprika meringue.

Note Cooking the custard in a water bath provides a gentle, even, and consistent heat. Place the baking dish on the oven shelf before filling it with boiling water from the kettle. It is safer and easier and prevents spilling.

Instant clear jel starch is a modified starch product often used in pie fillings. It is available online or from specialty baking stores.

Orange blossom tocinos
cielo with pear sorbet,
clove powder, and yuzu

CORDOBA OLIVE OIL ICE CREAM

Every country I have traveled in has claimed to have the best olive oil in the world and, to be honest, up until recently I believed that back home in Australia we produced some killer oils to rival anything else going around. Well, I can honestly say that after tasting Venta del Baron oil from Spain, it is the best I have ever experienced. I didn't want to mess with the grassy, fruity flavors of the oil, so I created this recipe to just complement the oil rather than overwhelm it.

You really do have to find the best olive oil possible for this dish. It just won't work with a poor quality olive oil. You'll need an ice cream maker for this recipe, too.

Beat the sugar and egg yolks together in the bowl of an electric stand mixer with a whisk attachment for 5 minutes until pale in color and thickened. Add the olive oil in a steady stream and continue beating for 3 minutes until smooth and airy. Add the milk, cream, vanilla seeds, and salt and whisk until combined. Pour into an ice cream maker and churn, then freeze according to the manufacturer's instructions.

Remove the ice cream from the freezer and leave to soften slightly before serving.

Note When making the custard base, ensure there are no lumps. Pass through a sieve to remove any lumps before churning. It is better to churn the ice cream when the custard is cool.

Olive oil ice cream

generous 1 cup (7¾ oz/220 g) sugar
6 egg yolks
⅓ cup (80 ml) olive oil
   (the best you can find)
3 cups (750 ml) milk
1 cup (250 ml) heavy cream
1 vanilla bean, split and seeds
   scraped
1 teaspoon sea salt

SMOKED CHIPOTLE AND CHOCOLATE FONDANT, SHERRY POACHED FIGS, AND ALMOND MILK ICE CREAM

Pedro Ximénez sherry and chocolate is one of the all-time classic matches. It just works. Pair that with a hot oozing chocolate fondant, a little kick from the smoked chipotle pepper, and the soothing touch of the almond milk ice cream, and you have all the makings of a knock-out dessert. And to be totally honest, my wife would kill me if I didn't put a fondant on the menu every year. So these ones are for you, Maha.

ALMOND MILK ICE CREAM

Preheat the oven to 400°F (200°C). Place the almonds on a small baking tray. Roast for 5–10 minutes. Remove and steep in the milk in a large bowl in the fridge overnight. Blend together in a food processor until the texture is smooth.

Place the sugar and almond milk in a saucepan over low heat to dissolve the sugar and combine. Remove from the heat and set aside.

Beat the egg yolks in an electric stand mixer with the whisk attachment at moderate–high speed for 5 minutes until thick and pale. Add the almond milk mixture and whisk well to combine.

Whip the cream to soft peaks in the stand mixer with the whisk attachment. Fold the almond mixture into the cream. Pour into a container and freeze for 2–3 hours.

PEDRO XIMÉNEZ POACHED FIGS

Put the sherry and sugar in a small saucepan over low heat and stir until the sugar has dissolved. Add the figs, cinnamon sticks, vanilla bean, and orange zest, and simmer for 10 minutes or until the figs are soft. Add the almonds, then remove from the heat.

Serve immediately or keep refrigerated for up to 1 week.

Almond milk ice cream

2 cups (10½ oz/300 g) blanched almonds

2 cups (500 ml) milk

½ cup (3½ oz/100 g) sugar

4 egg yolks

1 cup (250 ml) whipping cream

Sherry poached figs

1 cup (250 ml) Pedro Ximénez sherry

1¼ cups (9 oz/250 g) sugar

1 cup (4½ oz/125 g) dried white figs (or fresh figs when in season)

2 cinnamon sticks

1 vanilla bean, split and seeds scraped

zest of 1 orange

¾ cup (2¼ oz/60 g) roughly chopped roasted almonds

Smoked chipotle and bitter chocolate fondant

5½ oz (150 g) dark chocolate melting wafers (or dark chocolate chips)

1 teaspoon dried chipotle chili powder (see note)

11 tablespoons (5½ oz/150 g) butter, chopped, plus extra for greasing the molds

½ cup (120 ml) Pedro Ximénez sherry

3 eggs

3 egg yolks

¼ cup (2 oz/55 g) sugar

¼ cup (1¼ oz/35 g) all-purpose flour

SMOKED CHIPOTLE AND BITTER CHOCOLATE FONDANT

Melt the chocolate wafers, chipotle, and butter, stirring occasionally, in the top of a double boiler or in a heatproof bowl over simmering water until melted and glossy. Remove from the heat, add the Pedro Ximenex, and stir to combine. Set aside.

Beat the eggs, egg yolks, and sugar until thick and pale, sift in the flour, stir in the chocolate mixture, and mix gently to combine.

Grease six ½ cup (120 ml) metal baba molds with butter. Pour the mixture into the molds, cover with plastic wrap, and refrigerate for 2 hours or up to 5 days.

Preheat the oven to 400°F (200°C).

When ready to serve, remove the plastic wrap, then place the molds on a baking tray and bake for 10–12 minutes or until the puddings are firm around the edge. Remove from the oven and carefully run a knife around the edge of each mold, then turn the puddings out onto six plates.

TO SERVE

Remove the almond ice cream from the freezer and leave to soften slightly.

Serve the fondants with the poached figs and almond milk ice cream.

Notes Substitute canned chipotles in adobo sauce if chipotle powder is unavailable.

The fondants need to be just cooked and still soft and molten in the center. Check when cooking; the center will still look uncooked and the outside will be just set.

Smoked chipotle and
chocolate fondant, sherry
poached figs, and almond
milk ice cream

PANTRY

Aleppo pepper, also known as pul biber, is a mild chili flake used in Middle Eastern cooking. It has a mild heat and is available at specialist Middle Eastern grocery stores and online. If you can't find it, red pepper flakes or paprika are good substitutes.

Argan oil is a plant oil extract from the argan tree, which is native to Northern Africa. As well as being used in cooking, it is also used as a personal-care product. It is available from health food stores, select supermarkets, and online.

Brik pastry is available from specialty Middle Eastern grocery stores. If you have trouble finding it, use filo pastry instead.

Harissa is a North African hot chili paste made from roasted red peppers and a combination of herbs and spices. It is available at specialty Middle Eastern grocery stores and select supermarkets, as well as online.

Lamb tail fat is available from some butcher shops. Like other fats, it is solid at room temperature, but melts quickly with heat. Substitute suet or lard if necessary.

Liquid glucose, or glucose syrup, is a thick liquid sweetener made from starch. It is available at select supermarkets, as well as online.

Pomegranate molasses is the concentrated syrup of pomegranate juice. It is available at Middle Eastern grocery stores and select supermarkets, as well as online.

Preserved orange peel is available from specialty Middle Eastern grocery stores and select supermarkets, as well as online. If you can't find it, use preserved lemon peel.

Orange blossom water is the distilled by-product of bitter-orange blossoms. It is available at specialty Middle Eastern grocery stores and select supermarkets, as well as online.

Ras el hanout is a North African spice mix that comprises of a variety of spices, such as cardamom and cumin. It is available at specialty Middle Eastern grocery stores and select supermarkets, as well as online.

Red pepper paste is available at specialty food stores. It can also be purchased online. You can substitute a really good quality tomato paste.

Sabaht baharat (Lebanese 7 spice) is a Middle Eastern spice blend that usually consists of black pepper, cloves, cumin, nutmeg, coriander, cinnamon, and smoked paprika. It is available at specialty Middle Eastern grocery stores and select supermarkets, as well as online.

Saffron water is made by adding a pinch of saffron and 1 teaspoon of saffron powder to 4 cups (1 liter) of boiling water. It can also be purchased in cans at some Middle Eastern grocery stores.

Sucuk sausage is a Turkish sausage, usually made with beef, spiced with paprika and fenugreek. It can be purchased from continental delicatessens and specialty Middle Eastern grocery stores.

Sumac is a Middle Eastern spice made from dried, ground berries of a wild bush. It has a rich sour flavor. It is available at specialty Middle Eastern grocery stores, supermarkets, and online.

Tahini is a paste usually made from hulled sesame seeds. It can be found in the Middle Eastern section of supermarkets and specialty Middle Eastern grocery stores, as well as online.

Za'atar is a Middle Eastern spice blend that usually consists of dried wild thyme, sumac, marjoram, oregano, sesame seeds, and salt. It is available at specialist Middle Eastern grocery stores and can also be purchased online. If you can't find it, plain dried thyme is a good substitute.

INDEX

A

Aleppo pepper 266
ali nazik lamb kofte with eggplant yogurt and
black bread garnish 123
almond milk ice cream 262
almond purée 226, 236
Andalusia, Spain 214–19
apple pastilla 202–3
apple and watercress dressing 225
arak-cured kingfish with smashed radish dressing
32
argan oil 190, 266
argan oil chocolate mud brownie with orange
cinnamon ice cream 212
artichokes
artichoke and pea salad 242
roast Jerusalem artichokes 240

B

baklava 64, 65
barbecued pork ribs with fried eggplant and
molasses and smoked eggplant dip 255
beans
bissara with roasted garlic oil, scallops, carrots,
and cumin 171
fava bean salad 189
lamb shank kebab 116
beef
wagyu beef manti with peas, pickled onions, and
garlic yogurt 136
wagyu beef with roasted cauliflower hummus
and amlou dressing 190
wild greens with sucuk balls and eggs 131
beet mayonnaise 101
Beirut 26, 45
Bekaa Valley, Lebanon 54
bissara with roasted garlic oil, scallops, carrots and
cumin 171
black bread 124
black bread garnish 123
black garlic mayonnaise 150, 151
blackberry sorbet 154, 155
braised chickpea stew with lamb shank, eggplant,
and grains 175
braised lamb with saltbush and cantaloupe
132
braised pig's ears, morcilla, quail eggs, and jamon
236–7
braised rabbit with artichoke and pea salad
242–3
bread
black bread 124
black bread garnish 123
cumin flatbread 53
gremolata 186

nigella seed bread 82–3
pan-fried potato breads 182
preserved lemon and desert vegetable
medfouna 194
taramasalata 105
brik pastry 266
bulgur
bulgur dough 140
cracked wheat and tomato kibbeh 39
lamb and kishk kibbeh 42
brown butter 140

C

candied spiced pumpkin 61
caramel
caramelized onion dressing 236
salted tahini caramel 64, 65
carob 58
carrots 171
carrot and preserved orange purée 193
sardine kefta with fresh chermoula salad 181
cauliflower: wagyu beef with roasted cauliflower
hummus and amlou dressing 190
cemen-cured blue eye pastirma with taramasalata
105
cheese
feta borek 106
grilled haloumi with pomegranate and sumac
dressing 35
morel, Swiss chard, and duck gozleme with
morel butter 112
pastirma, shrimp, and feta pide 120
ricotta and carob lady fingers 58
chermoula paste 181
chicken
chicken cornbread dumpling soup 148
harira soup with pan-fried chicken dumplings
and fava bean salad 189
quail egg kefta tabriz 81
saffron marinated chicken 172
stuffed chicken wings with sour cherry barbecue
sauce 45
chickpeas
braised chickpea stew with lamb shank,
eggplant, and grains 175
hummus 53
quail egg kefta tabriz 81
roast chickpea hummus with lamb kebab 139
wagyu beef with roasted cauliflower hummus
and amlou dressing 190
chili
pickled eggplants with black pepper and green
chili 76
smoked chipotle and chocolate fondant, sherry
poached figs, and almond milk ice cream 262–3

chocolate
argan oil chocolate mud brownie with orange
cinnamon ice cream 212
chocolate and pistachio m'hencha 206
salted white chocolate ice cream 211
smoked chipotle and chocolate fondant, sherry
poached figs, and almond milk ice cream 262–3
cinnamon sugar 65
clementine and saffron marmalade 199
clove cookie crumbs 256, 257
Cordoba olive oil ice cream 260
cornbread 150
cornbread and fennel seed coated sardines 144
couscous
foot of the mountain couscous with garden
vegetables 178
shellfish moghrabieh 36
cracked wheat and tomato kibbeh 39
cumin flatbread 53
cured salmon with beet mayonnaise, pumpkin
purée, and fennel vinaigrette 101

D

date, orange, and olive oil cake with salted white
chocolate ice cream 211
date and ras el hanout ice cream 202
desserts see sweet things
dip, smoked eggplant 255
doughnuts, pistachio and barberry nougat, with
orange blossom syrup 90
dressings
apple and watercress dressing 225
beet mayonnaise 101
black garlic mayonnaise 150, 151
caramelized onion dressing 236
fennel vinaigrette 101
garlic yogurt 136, 140
gazpacho-flavored mayonnaise 230
harissa aioli 222
herbed crème fraîche 147
mustard mayonnaise 16, 17
preserved lemon dressing 109
roast garlic vinaigrette 87
sherry dressing 227
smashed radish dressing 32
smoked eel dressing 102
smoked eggplant mayonnaise 106
duck
duck awarma 50
duck fat 50
freekeh risotto with duck awarma, poached eggs,
and toasted nuts 54
hummus, duck awarma, and cumin flatbreads 53
morel, Swiss chard, and duck gozleme with
morel butter 112

tea-smoked duck with kale and hazelnut salad 150–1

dumplings
chicken cornbread dumpling soup 148
harira soup with pan-fried chicken dumplings and fava bean salad 189

E

eggplant
ali nazik lamb kofte with eggplant yogurt and black bread garnish 123
barbecued pork ribs with fried eggplant and molasses and smoked eggplant dip 255
braised chickpea stew with lamb shank, eggplant, and grains 175
lamb shoulder with potato and eggplant tagine 186
pickled eggplants with black pepper and green chili 76
smoked eggplant mayonnaise 106

eggs
braised pig's ears, morcilla, quail eggs, and jamon 236–7
freekeh risotto with duck awarma, poached eggs, and toasted nuts 54
pickled quail eggs 226
quail egg kefta tabriz 81
wild greens with sucuk balls and eggs 131

F

fava bean salad 189
fennel vinaigrette 101
fenugreek salad 87
feta borek 106
figs
fig and walnut ice cream 62
Pedro Ximénez poached figs 262
vine leaf-wrapped quail, sucuk, and candied walnuts and figs 127
fish
arak-cured kingfish with smashed radish dressing 32
cemen-cured blue eye pastirma with taramasalata 105
cornbread and fennel seed coated sardines 144
cured salmon with beet mayonnaise, pumpkin purée, and fennel vinaigrette 101
sardine kefta with fresh chermoula salad 181
sardine and preserved orange rice pilaf with herbed crème fraîche 147
smoked trout trahana 115
taramasalata 105
tuna tartare, harissa aioli 222
see also seafood

foot of the mountain couscous with garden vegetables 178
freekeh
braised chickpea stew with lamb shank, eggplant, and grains 175
freekeh risotto with duck awarma, poached eggs, and toasted nuts 54
fries, spicy Dahlia 46
frozen peanut butter parfait, salted tahini caramel, and broken baklava 64–5

G

Gallipoli Campaign 96
garden vegetables with foot of the mountain couscous 178
garlic
black garlic mayonnaise 150, 151
braised lamb with saltbush and cantaloupe 132
garlic yogurt 136, 140
lamb shank kebab 116
pickled eggplants with black pepper and green chili 76
roast garlic vinaigrette 87
slow-roasted lamb shoulder 82
garnish, black bread 123
gazpacho-flavored mayonnaise 230
glucose syrup 266
gozleme dough 112
gremolata 186

H

haloumi, grilled, with pomegranate and sumac dressing 35
harira soup with pan-fried chicken dumplings and fava bean salad 189
harissa 266
harissa aioli 222
herbed crème fraîche 147
hummus 53
roast chickpea hummus with lamb kebab 139
roasted cauliflower hummus 190

I

ice cream
almond milk ice cream 262
Cordoba olive oil ice cream 260
date and ras el hanout ice cream 202
fig and walnut ice cream 62
orange cinnamon ice cream 212
salted white chocolate ice cream 211
icli kofte with garlic yogurt and brown butter 140
Iran 68–73
Istanbul 96

J

Jerusalem artichokes, roast 240

K

kale and hazelnut salad 150, 151
kangaroo tail with roast Jerusalem artichokes 240
kebab
lamb shank kebab 116
roast chickpea hummus with lamb kebab 139
kefta
quail egg kefta tabriz 81
sardine kefta with fresh chermoula salad 181
kibbeh
cracked wheat and tomato kibbeh 39
lamb and kishk kibbeh 42
kofte
ali nazik lamb kofte with eggplant yogurt and black bread garnish 123
icli kofte with garlic yogurt and brown butter 140

L

lamb
ali nazik lamb kofte with eggplant yogurt and black bread garnish 123
braised chickpea stew with lamb shank, eggplant, and grains 175
braised lamb with saltbush and cantaloupe 132
lamb and kishk kibbeh 42
lamb sfiha 57
lamb shank kebab 116
lamb shoulder with potato and eggplant tagine 186
lamb tail fat 266
quail egg kefta tabriz 81
roast chickpea hummus with lamb kebab 139
slow-roasted lamb shoulder with nomad's jeweled yogurt and nigella seed bread 82–3
wild greens with sucuk balls and eggs 131
Lebanese 7 spice 266
Lebanon 24–7
lemon
preserved lemon and desert vegetable medfouna 194
preserved lemon dressing 109

M

Maha 6
Malta 10–15, 96
manti dough 136
marmalade, clementine, and saffron 199
Marrakesh 167
mastic pudding with chocolate soil, blackberry sorbet, and rosemary pearls 154–5
meat curing 105

melon: braised lamb with saltbush and cantaloupe 132

mint and apple pastilla with date and ras el hanout ice cream 202–3

mint crème 202

Moorish chilled almond and orange blossom soup with apple and watercress dressing 225

morel, Swiss chard, and duck gozleme with morel butter 112

Morocco 162–7, 216

mustard mayonnaise 16, 17

N

nigella seed bread 82–3

nomad's jeweled yogurt 82

nougat, pistachio and barberry 90

O

olive oil poached potatoes, pickled octopus, and green olives 235

onions

    caramelized onion dressing 236

    couscous with onion 36

    lamb kebabs 139

    rabo de kangaroo 240

    red onion salad 139

orange

    clementine and saffron marmalade 199

    date, orange, and olive oil cake with salted white chocolate ice cream 211

    orange blossom syrup 90

    orange blossom tocinos cielo with pear sorbet, clove powder, and yuzu 256–7

    orange blossom water 266

    orange cinnamon ice cream 212

    orange and coriander crumb 102

    orange grove beghrir with orange blossom yogurt 200

    preserved orange peel 266

    sardine and preserved orange rice pilaf with herbed crème fraîche 147

Ottoman Empire 96

P

pan-fried potato breads 182

paprika meringue 256, 257

pastirma, shrimp, and feta pide 120

pastizzi 16, 17

    pork and pea pastizzi with mustard mayonnaise 16–17

pastry

    chocolate and pistachio m'hencha 206

    gozleme 112

    mint and apple pastilla with date and ras el hanout ice cream 202–3

    pastirma, shrimp, and feta pide 120

    ricotta and carob lady fingers 58

salt-crusted fruits of the sea with jamon and sherry cream 252

peaches, saffron-roasted, with saffron cotton candy 93

peanut butter parfait 64

pear sorbet 256

peas

    artichoke and pea salad 242

    pork and pea pastizzi with mustard mayonnaise 16–17

Persian food 70, 73

pickles

    pickled eggplants with black pepper and green chili 76

    pickled octopus 235

pide, pastirma, shrimp, and feta 120

pistachio and barberry nougat doughnuts with orange blossom syrup 90

pistachio crumble 158

poached lobster pringa with gazpacho-flavored mayonnaise and crispy shrimp 230

pomegranate molasses 266

pork

    barbecued pork ribs with fried eggplant and molasses and smoked eggplant dip 255

    braised pig's ears, morcilla, quail eggs, and jamon 236–7

    pork and pea pastizzi with mustard mayonnaise 16–17

    roasted pork belly with fenugreek salad and roast garlic vinaigrette 87

    tortillas de camarones and pork belly on brioche buns 249

potatoes

    lamb shoulder with potato and eggplant tagine 186

    olive oil poached potatoes, pickled octopus, and green olives 235

    pan-fried potato breads 182

    quail egg kefta tabriz 81

    spicy Dahlia fries 46

preserved lemon and desert vegetable medfouna 194

preserved lemon dressing 109

preserved orange peel 266

pumpkin

    candied spiced pumpkin 61

    pumpkin purée 101

    pumpkin Turkish delight 161

Q

quail eggs

    braised pig's ears, morcilla, quail eggs, and jamon 236–7

    pickled quail eggs 226

    quail egg kefta tabriz 81

quail, sucuk, and candied walnuts and figs, vine leaf-wrapped 127

R

rabbit

    braised rabbit with artichoke and pea salad 242–3

    rabbit stew with raisin gremolata 21

rabo de kangaroo with roast jerusalem artichokes 240

radish: smashed radish dressing 32

raisin gremolata 21

ras el hanout 266

red onion salad 139

red pepper paste 266

rfissa 172

rice

    braised chickpea stew with lamb shank, eggplant, and grains 175

    rosewater sutlac with pistachio crumble 158

    sardine and preserved orange rice pilaf with herbed crème fraîche 147

    squid ink rice with chorizo-filled baby calamari and seaweed 246

    stuffed mussels with preserved lemon dressing 109

    vine leaf-wrapped quail, sucuk, and candied walnuts and figs 127

ricotta and carob lady fingers 58

risotto, freekeh, with duck awarma, poached eggs, and toasted nuts 54

roast chickpea hummus with lamb kebab 139

roasted pork belly with fenugreek salad and roast garlic vinaigrette 87

rosemary pearls 154

rosewater sutlac with pistachio crumble 158

S

sabaht baharat 266

saffron 93

    clementine and saffron marmalade 199

    saffron marinated chicken 172

    saffron-roasted peaches with saffron cotton candy 93

    saffron water 266

    veal shank and saffron with carrot and preserved orange purée 193

salads

    artichoke and pea salad 242

    fava bean salad 189

    fenugreek salad 87

    fresh chermoula salad 181

    kale and hazelnut salad 150, 151

    red onion salad 139

salmorejo with jamon, quail egg, green apple, and sherry dressing 226–7

salt-crusted fruits of the sea with jamon and sherry cream 252

salted white chocolate ice cream 211

sardine kefta with fresh chermoula salad 181

sardine and preserved orange rice pilaf with herbed crème fraîche 147 scallop-filled zucchini flowers with smoked eel dressing and orange and coriander crumb 102

seafood
bissara with roasted garlic oil, scallops, carrots, and cumin 171
Moorish chilled almond and orange blossom soup with apple and watercress dressing 225
olive oil poached potatoes, pickled octopus, and green olives 235
pastirma, shrimp, and feta pide 120
poached lobster pringa with gazpacho-flavored mayonnaise and crispy shrimp 230
salt-crusted fruits of the sea with jamon and sherry cream 252
scallop-filled zucchini flowers with smoked eel dressing and orange and coriander crumb 102
shellfish moghrabieh 36
sherry poached figs 262
smoked eel dressing 102
squid ink rice with chorizo-filled baby calamari and seaweed 246
stuffed mussels with preserved lemon dressing 109
tortillas de camarones and pork belly on brioche buns 249
see also fish
salted tahini caramel 64, 65
semolina: orange grove beghrir with orange blossom yogurt 200
shellfish moghrabieh 36
sherry dressing 227

shrimp
Moorish chilled almond and orange blossom soup with apple and watercress dressing 225
pastirma, shrimp, and feta pide 120

soup
chicken cornbread dumpling soup 148
harira soup with pan-fried chicken dumplings and fava bean salad 189
Moorish chilled almond and orange blossom soup with apple and watercress dressing 225
sour cherry barbecue sauce 45
spiced wafer 222
squid ink rice with chorizo-filled baby calamari and seaweed 246
stuffed chicken wings with sour cherry barbecue sauce 45
stuffed mussels with preserved lemon dressing 109
sucuk sausage 266
vine leaf-wrapped quail, sucuk, and candied walnuts and figs 127
wild greens with sucuk balls and eggs 131
sugar syrup 161
sumac 266

sweet things
argan oil chocolate mud brownie with orange cinnamon ice cream 212

chocolate and pistachio m'hencha 206
Cordoba olive oil ice cream 260
date, orange, and olive oil cake with salted white chocolate ice cream 211
date and ras el hanout ice cream 202
fig and walnut ice cream 62
frozen peanut butter parfait, salted tahini caramel, and broken baklava 64–5
mastic pudding with chocolate soil, blackberry sorbet, and rosemary pearls 154–5
mint and apple pastilla with date and ras el hanout ice cream 202–3
mint crème 202
orange blossom tocinos cielo with pear sorbet, clove powder, and yuzu 256–7
paprika meringue 256, 257
pistachio and barberry nougat doughnuts with orange blossom syrup 90
pumpkin Turkish delight 161
rosewater sutlac with pistachio crumble 158
saffron-roasted peaches with saffron cotton candy 93
smoked chipotle and chocolate fondant, sherry poached figs, and almond milk ice cream 262–3

Swiss chard
morel, Swiss chard, and duck gozleme with morel butter 112
wild greens with sucuk balls and eggs 131
slow-roasted lamb shoulder with nomad's jeweled yogurt and nigella seed bread 82–3
smashed radish dressing 32
smoked chipotle and chocolate fondant, sherry poached figs, and almond milk ice cream 262–3
smoked eel dressing 102
smoked eggplant dip 255
smoked eggplant mayonnaise 106
smoked trout trahana 115

T
tahini 266
taramasalata 105
tea-smoked duck with kale and hazelnut salad 150–1
tempura batter 109

tomatoes
cracked wheat and tomato kibbeh 39
lamb and kishk kibbeh 42
lamb shank kebab 116
salmorejo purée 226
tortillas de camarones and pork belly on brioche buns 249
tuna tartare, harissa aioli 222
Turkey 94–9

V
veal shank and saffron with carrot and preserved orange purée 193

vegetables
foot of the mountain couscous with garden vegetables 178
preserved lemon and desert vegetable medfouna 194
vegetable stock 178
village-style feta borek with smoked eggplant mayonnaise 106
vine leaf-wrapped quail, sucuk, and candied walnuts and figs 127

W
wagyu beef manti with peas, pickled onions, and garlic yogurt 136
wagyu beef with roasted cauliflower hummus and amlou dressing 190

walnuts
fig and walnut ice cream 62
gremolata 186
lamb shank kebab 116
vine leaf-wrapped quail, sucuk, and candied walnuts and figs 127
wild greens with sucuk balls and eggs 131

Y
yogurt
eggplant yogurt 123
garlic yogurt 136, 140
nomad's jeweled yogurt 82
orange grove beghrir with orange blossom yogurt 200
yuzu purée 256, 257

Z
za'atar 266
zucchini flowers, scallop-filled, with smoked eel dressing and orange and coriander crumb 102

First published in 2017 by

INTERLINK BOOKS
An imprint of Interlink Publishing Group, Inc.
46 Crosby Street, Northampton, Massachusetts 01060
www.interlinkbooks.com

Australian Publisher: Jane Morrow
American Publisher: Michel Moushabeck
Design Manager: Megan Pigott
Designer: Jacqui Porter
Editor: Emma Hutchinson
American Edition Editor: Leyla Moushabeck
Food Editor and Stylist: Caroline Velik
Photographer: Rob Palmer
Food Preparation: Petros Dellidis
Production Manager: Alexandra Gonzalez

Library of Congress Cataloging-in-Publication Data available.

ISBN 978-1-56656-006-1

Color reproduction by Splitting Image Color Studio Pty Ltd, Clayton, Victoria
Printed by 1010 Printing International Limited, China

To request our complete 48-page, full-color catalog, please call us toll free at 1-800-238-LINK,
visit our website at www.interlinkbooks.com, or send us an e-mail: info@interlinkbooks.com.

Those who might be at risk from the effects
of salmonella poisoning (the elderly, pregnant
women, young children, and those suffering from
immune deficiency diseases) should consult their
doctor with any concerns about eating raw or
undercooked foods.